On The Way To

Death

Essays Toward a Comic Vision

Books by A. Roy Eckardt

Christianity and the Children of Israel

The Surge of Piety in America

Elder and Younger Brothers

The Theologian at Work (editor)

Christianity in Israel (editor)

Your People, My People

Jews and Christians

For Righteousness' Sake

Black-Woman-Jew

Reclaiming the Jesus of History

Sitting in the Earth and Laughing

Collecting Myself (ed. Alice L. Eckardt)

No Longer Aliens, No Longer Strangers

How To Tell God From the Devil

On the Way to Death

Comic and Ethicist (forthcoming)

By Alice L. Eckardt and A. Roy Eckardt

Encounter With Israel

Long Night's Journey Into Day

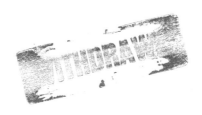

On The Way To

Death

Essays Toward a Comic Vision

A. Roy Eckardt

TRANSACTION PUBLISHERS
New Brunswick (U.S.A.) and London (U.K.)

2.36.1
E 19o

All rights reserved under International and Pan-American Copyright Conventions. No part of this book may be reproduced or transmitted in any form or by any means, electronic or mechanical, including photocopy, recording, or any information storage and retrieval system, without prior permission in writing from the publisher. All inquiries should be addressed to Transaction Publishers, Rutgers—The State University, New Brunswick, New Jersey 08903.

This book is printed on acid-free paper that meets the American National Standard for Permanence of Paper for Printed Library Materials.

Library of Congress Catalog Number: 95-37826
ISBN: 1-56000-234-4
Printed in the United States of America

Library of Congress Cataloging-in-Publication Data

Eckardt, A. Roy (Arthur Roy), 1918–
    On the way to death : essays toward a comic vision / A. roy Eckardt.
        p. cm.
    Includes bibliographical references and index.
    ISBN 1-56000-234-4 (alk. paper)
    1. Comic, The—Religious aspects—Christianity.   2. Death—Religious aspects—Christianity.k.   I. Title.
BR115.C63E24   1995
236'.1—dc20   95-37826
                                                                      CIP

For three I have loved, differently

Robert Frederick William Eckardt
1915–1940
(My brother Robbie)

Mary of Magdala
(Who continued to weep)

Angelo Giuseppe Roncalli
1881–1963
(Good Pope John XXIII)

Human beings are sojourners on the way to death.
—Wendy Farley

The Devil is very old.
—Johann Wolfgang von Goethe

Angels, spirits, principalities, powers, gods,
Satan—these, along with all other spiritual
realities, are the unmentionables of our culture.
—Walter Wink

History is thorough, and passes through many
phases when it ushers an old form to the grave. The
final phase of a world-historical form is its comedy.
—Karl Marx

The shadow of death that looms over tragedy
lifts when it is comedy's turn, leaving in place the
mad buoyancy of life, an urgency that jostles but
does not kill.
—Marcel Gutwirth

Contents

Preface

I tender my appreciation to President Philip Alexander and the staff of the Centre for Hebrew and Jewish Studies, Oxford University, where I prepared most of this book. I also thank my friend Marion Clump for certain linguistic counsel. In addition, I am much indebted to Lynn Guarente and Laurence Mintz, my editors at Transaction. Most of all, I express my gratitude to my wife Alice L. Eckardt for help that only I can know.

Unless otherwise indicated, biblical citations are taken from the *New Revised Standard Version (NRSV)*.

A. ROY ECKARDT
Easter Monday 1994

Introduction

This study is the final part of a trilogy. Earlier parts are *Sitting in the Earth and Laughing: A Handbook of Humor* and *How To Tell God From the Devil: On the Way to Comedy*.[1] The first of these is at once a serious guide to the reality of humor and an exemplification of humor itself. The second volume presents the thesis that a particular rendering of "the comic vision"[2] may offer a creative way to reckon with the practical promise of the book's title. This third part seeks to relate the domain of comedy to the subject of God in the context of the question of death. Since I wrote *Sitting in the Earth*, I have come to prefer the (for me, broader and deeper) terms *comedy* and *the comic* to *humor* and *humorous*.

The standpoint throughout the study, as in the other two sections of the trilogy is, primarily, the history of ideas tempered by a premodernist/ postmodernist commitment that pledges neither to sacrifice matter to spirit nor spirit to matter. I take a partial bow to Walter Wink and his own trilogy dealing with "the Powers."[3] I do not imply that either of us would agree with everything the other says. Wink rescues the concept and reality of power and the Powers from the non-New Testament attempt to reduce them from a human/political dimension to a purely "spiritual" dimension, as at the same time he authenticates their spiritual quality and integrity. It is unfortunate that, despite his forceful recognition of the horrors of evil, Professor Wink cannot *quite* bring himself to subsume the Devil within God Godself (a residue of the modernist enlightenment he otherwise effectively criticizes?). Thus, he elevates *human* "choices" and *human* "responses to the satanic occasion" to be "the determining factor in how Satan is constellated": whether as "Servant"

1

of God or as "Evil One."[4] This serious theological-ethical fault is already opposed in my *How To Tell God From the Devil* and will be intensively dealt with through the pages that follow, wherein it is maintained that God is the One who determines the constellation of the Devil, when the Devil is operative as radical evil. (I nowhere suggest that we humans are free of responsibility for fighting radical evil.)

Within my recent writing upon the triad Comedy/God/Devil I pursue a goal somewhat overlapping that of Walter Wink, although with different points of departure, procedure, and outcome. Of late, I have had quite a bit to say on the first and the third of the variables listed. The volume before the reader concentrates upon the second one—but is God a variable?—though with aid from the first and the third.

One of the epigraphs at the beginning of this book could also operate as an epitaph. In a work introductory of Hegel, Karl Marx declares: "History is thorough, and passes through many phases when it ushers an old form to the grave. The final phase of a world-historical form is its comedy."[5] Marx is referring, of course, to collective history, and it is as a hostile witness that he does this. In contrast, I apply his words to the condition of the individual, and I am being descriptive and normative, perhaps even celebrative. Again, it is at the start of his introduction that Marx's famous judgment is found, "the critique of religion is the prerequisite of every critique."[6] This can be readily offered as an additional epigraph (epitaph?) within or to my own work through the years, inclusive of *On the Way to Death.*

Notes

1. A. Roy Eckardt, *Sitting in the Earth and Laughing* (New Brunswick and London: Transaction Publishers, Rutgers University, 1992); *How To Tell God From the Devil* (New Brunswick and London: Transaction Publishers, Rutgers University, 1995).
2. See Edward L. Galligan, *The Comic Vision in Literature* (Athens: University of Georgia, 1984).
3. Walter Wink, *Naming the Powers: The Language of Power in the New Testament* (Philadelphia: Fortress Press, 1984); *Unmasking the Powers: The Invisible Forces That Determine Human Existence* (Philadelphia: Fortress Press, 1986); and *Engaging the Powers: Discernment and Resistance in a World of Domination* (Minneapolis: Fortress Press, 1992).
4. See especially Wink, *Unmasking the Powers,* 30-39. Wink is particularly convincing in naming the Powers as at once *"the outer and inner aspects of one and the same concretion of power.* 'Spiritual' here means the inner dimension of the

material, the 'within' of things, the subjectivity of objective entities in the world" (*Naming the Powers*, 107). On the other hand and against Wink, just because, as he elsewhere points out, the first Christians did not blame God "for their unmerited sufferings" (*Engaging the Powers*, 316), this does not mean that we today ought to be so lacking in human dignity. Whom else but God is to be blamed? Again, we are told by Wink that Jesus was "executed by God's servants" (*Naming the Powers*, 114). I offer quite an alternative historical finding in *Reclaiming the Jesus of History* (Minneapolis: Fortress Press, 1992). See also Wink, *Engaging the Powers*, 109-10, 139-40, 147-48.

5. Karl Marx, "A Contribution to the Critique of Hegel's 'Philosophy of Right,' Introduction," in *Critique of Hegel's "Philosophy of Right,"* trans. Annette Jolin and Joseph O'Malley, ed. O'Malley (Cambridge: Cambridge University Press, 1970), 134, slightly emended. In answer to his own question, "Why does history proceed in this way?" Marx explains: "So that mankind will separate itself happily from its past."
6. Ibid., 132.

Part I

Foundations

1

The Ugliest Customer

There is no such thing as dying with dignity.
—Paul Ramsey

Why, in the presence of God, is there death?
—G. Tom Milazzo

Insofar as comedy bespeaks incongruity (one major and persisting interpretation of what makes comedy comedy), death as the final incongruity of life may be received as essentially comic and, hence, as open to response and study from that same point of view.

I

I have reached a stage where I am beginning, at least ideationally (the religious people would want to say "spiritually," a word I have always found hard to understand) to prepare for my own death. Some three-quarters of a century of self-sufficiency and self-care may have begun to run out of steam.

Morbid, isn't he?

No, he is not. All living things will one day die, including all those yet to be born, indeed every precious baby being delivered at this very moment. It is quite wrongheaded to associate morbidness with such a *universal* condition/future as this. The condition may be *sad* all right, but its affirmation is not morbid—unless we are to adjudge that *everything* demands that description.

We have to be severely on guard against the notion that older people (let us say those over sixty-five) have now come to the virtual end of

7

"real" life, with everything downhill from there on. In her book *The Fountain of Age*, Betty Friedan effectively rejects this Mystique of Age, as she once attacked the Feminine Mystique.[1] An ideology opposite to the Mystique of Age, yet equally untenable, is the Negation of Death. For all their difference, the two ideologies converge in and through our dominating cult of youth, wherein age and death are together denied.

In *Of Truth* Francis Bacon concludes that, having asked "What is truth?" jesting Pilate "would not stay for an answer." I assume in these pages that jesting is acceptable when it is intrepid enough and/or patient enough to stay around and sustain the search for truth. *I am not completely sure when I shall be jesting and when not.* At the start of chapter 6, I submit a brief defense of the suddenness of some of my shifts from comedy to noncomedy and back again. One useful rule of thumb is that the comedy and even nonsense (a respectable branch of comedy) I purvey throughout these pages is, paradoxically, a sign of earnestness. I suppose this implies that the noncomedy I here and there dispense (the academic and/or theoretical, i.e., more congruous, material) may not always come up to that reputable, earnest level. Withal, this study as a whole mirrors the same anguish as that of the father-forsaken child who demands to know, "Is Daddy ever going to come home?" (Will God ever come out of the darkness and the silence to abide with us?) Comedy is a most serious, sometimes even desperate, business—Joan Rivers identifies herself as a "walking wound," owning up that her routines come out of total unhappiness[2]—and the humor of any individual confronting death (or just *imagining* her or his death) is transcendingly earnest.

The anticipation of death brings suffering to human beings, quite independently of the act of dying itself. On one occasion Brother Elias told Francis of Assisi of a dream wherein a certain priest ordered him to find Francis and tell him that within two years he would die. Francis's response (to his own physician) was: "Thanks be to God. I am not a coward who fears death."[3] All right, so I'm a coward—yet so, perhaps, are more than a few of my readers. I want to be able to communicate with them—with you. According to Eric W. Gritsch, all the evidence suggests that it was the fear of death that drove Martin Luther into the monastic life.[4]

There is no suggestion here or anywhere in this book that suffering cannot sometimes be redemptive. In my late years I am of course made particularly aware that "human beings are sojourners on the way to death."[5] There may well be elements of hypocrisy and immorality in a person of my age and objective comfortableness taking literary aim at death—in the presence (or absence) of those poor souls who, with my own brother, have died young, or who go on living but suffer so much more than I (a living death). Unfortunately, awareness of this comparative condition does little to offset the terror. You could say, I guess, that what I am actually doing as I write this book is playing the percentages, while of course hoping that, in my case as in yours (even though you remain unknown to me), the percentages may somehow go away: The average life expectancy for today's white American male is seventy-five (much lower for black males—pointing again to the phenomenon of hypocrisy, not to mention ideology). Since, as I write, I am more or less at the appropriate age for dying, it would appear that, statistically or nomothetically speaking, though not idiographically, I have a fifty-fifty chance of living to finish this book. Idiographically, I either have every chance or no chance at all.[6]

Having satisfied a little the spirit of *mea culpa*, I turn to a source that captures what is, I hope, the *esprit* of my book (for the French, *esprit* signifies both mind and wit, though above all, courtesy): Søren Kierkegaard attests that "the more one suffers, the more...has one a sense for the Comic. It is only by the deepest suffering that one acquires true authority in the use of the comic, an authority which by one word transforms as by magic the reasonable creature one calls man into a caricature."[7]

If the comic is in essence a caricature, is not death the final caricature? Here develops the inner, incredible link between comedy/humor and the end of all things earthly. (Think of the glorious musical send-offs of "the saints" in our blessed City of New Orleans, a glory whose pain is veiled but stays no less severe.[8])

Among the explorations in these pages is the hypothesis that faith (trust and hope) possibly helps to bond, and thereby to assimilate, the question of suffering to the question of comedy. Accordingly, "the life journey of God"—part II of this study, and the book's intended apogee—is a life-and-death affair for me, which may help explain why I not only take (irresponsible? I should prefer to say "mischievous") refuge in elements of humor as the exposition proceeds but later go so far as to associate redemption from death itself with comedy.

Yet no magical powers are to be found in comedy. Comedy is as problematic as any and every human endeavor. To idealize comedy is to forget its prevalent submission to evil causes—as in the historic and abiding utilization of humor by males in the oppression of females.[9] Even were we to characterize this practice as a distortion of an essentially good phenomenon, the truth remains that, beyond their critical functions, humor and comedy manifest a strong tendency to serve the status quo, to be "predominantly a conservative, rather than liberating or constructive, force in society."[10]

If comedy and humor are problematic to the human condition, so is faith. In *The Protest and the Silence* G. Tom Milazzo writes that faith proceeds, not from concepts, but "from the encounter between the presence of the divine and the human. As long as this encounter occurs within the realm of human existence, it is necessarily problematic."[11] But the trouble is that faith is itself a lot more problematic than Milazzo here allows. In truth, faith proceeds from a mere slender human *affirmation* of an *alleged* encounter between the presence of the divine, on the one side, and the human dimension as such, on the other side. For the "presence of the divine" is itself wholly problematic—as Milazzo is quick to recognize close by.[12]

I interpret God as the One I am to meet, the One we are to meet: the Final Presence (*Shekinah*). Yet this too involves at best a human declaration or hope; *the interpretation can make no assured claim to facticity.* May not the Final Presence be in reality a Final Absence? Much more important, within the context of death the terrible anguish intrudes: Who can be entirely certain that God is worth meeting?

> *God:* How do you do?
> *Human:* You will have to excuse me.
>   I have business and concerns elsewhere.

II

William Hazlitt called death "the ugly customer." He ought to have said "ugliest," since death is the one destruction that is certain, universal, and unexceptional, the one Absolute that suffuses finite existence. (Death has been teamed with taxes to comprise life's two supposed certainties. The linkage is insulting; before the advent of death, the act of paying one's taxes is to be numbered among life's many joys—granted you have the money and the taxes are just.)

Ernest Becker tells it as it is: "Existence, for all organismic life, is a constant struggle to feed—a struggle to incorporate whatever other organisms they can fit into their mouths and press down their gullets without choking. Seen in these stark terms, life on this planet is a gory spectacle, a science-fiction nightmare in which digestive tracts fitted with teeth at one end are tearing away at whatever flesh they can reach, and at the other end are piling up the fuming waste excrement as they move along in search of more flesh."[13]

You and I are responsible for many deaths. But we who feed upon others are soon fed upon. "Of all things that move man one of the principal ones is his terror of death." For "underneath the most bland exterior lurks the universal anxiety, the 'worm at the core,'" that "layer of our true and basic animal anxieties, the terror that we carry around in our secret heart."[14] The fears of life may be great, but they are as nothing before the terror of death.

For fairness' sake, we do well to take into account the contention of Daphne Hampson (in which she is not alone) that "the male sense of self (typically)" makes men "more liable to be prone to *Angst*" ("anxiety without an object"), that "they think differently than do women about sacrifice and death, and that it matters more to them that there should be a continuation in eternal life." Hampson reasons that the male concern with immortality "seems to come out of a control instinct—such that one would, if one could, also control what happens to one's individual self the other side of death.... It may be because women live, to a greater extent than do many men, in a web of relations with others that *Angst* may not be such a dominant theme in their lives."[15]

Insofar as a life/death incongruity is interpretable as crucial within the etiology of comedy, I should hate to see Hampson's differentiation contribute to a revival of the discredited stereotype of women as having "less than" the sense of humor and comedy that men possess. Equally important, it is the case that whenever in this study I allude to the terror of death, I mean not simply one's individual death but the deaths of loved ones. These deaths can be more terrible than the portent of one's own demise.

One of the most terrifying powers of death is its ability, with Nature and/or human beings as its tools, to create horror out of its own horror.

In August of 1993 the Missouri River came through Hardin, Missouri—located an ostensibly safe five miles north of the river—and excavated a tremendous crater, carrying away the town's entire cemetery. Close to 900 bodies, caskets, and burial vaults were swept downstream toward Saint Louis and the Mississippi. One witness reported that it was as if the dead had died all over again and the survivors were compelled to grieve anew. Birthdays, anniversaries, and other reminders do not seem to satisfy the insatiable appetite of Death for human suffering. A retired nurse wanted to know, "What is God saying to us? What is it we're doing that we shouldn't be doing?"[16] Death is more than a matter of fact. Death is an incarnation of cruelty.

Mark Taylor somewhere makes the point that death is so disastrous exactly because it is always approaching yet never arriving. I take it he means that once it arrives, the disaster is over. I should want to interject that this finding applies at best only to the individual who dies. For those who are left behind, the disaster *is* the actual arrival of death together with the pain that refuses to go away. I think of my wife, my children, my friends, and other loved ones. Why should *they* have to endure my death? *Why must I do such a thing to them?* (Why should they be forced to do such a thing to me?) This itself is to be numbered among the terrors of death.

III

What, if anything, or who, if anyone, is responsible for death, that terror of terrors?

An "anything" would be responsible (i.e., causative), yet not blameworthy. An "anyone" would be not alone responsible but also culpable (*strafwürdig*). What makes the dialectic of death so enigmatic, existentially as much as intellectually, is that death is at once *natural*, a perfectly everyday, ordinary phenomenon, and *moral/immoral*, a matter of most singular and agonizing judgment, even of revulsion.

One party we sometimes subpeona to account for death is Nature. For, applied to humankind, it is Nature that issues the decree: "Every single human being exists in order to perish some day," just as humanity "as a whole will disappear as well as the planet it inhabits, the Sun around which this planet orbits, even the galaxy in which this Sun is located."[17] Something might be said for the notion that it is Nature that constitutes the (unconscious) source of our final nemesis, on the basis that many of us find it easier to endure a universe indifferent to our fate than one that is hostile to us, consciously decreeing our eventual extinction. Nevertheless, Nature as an explanation is too superficial to be satisfactory. We seem driven to ask, to know: Who is it or at least what is it that lurks *behind* Nature's unknowing destructiveness? (Only a single one of the countless diseases persistently afflicting humankind has ever been completely eradicated: smallpox.)

In the Western tradition extra-natural accountings have entailed one or both of two major foci: God and the Devil. These worthies (*sic*) compete for blameworthiness. If God is Lord of life (*haim*), where does this leave God respecting the reality of death (*mot*)? The psalmist places humankind's "seventy years, or perhaps eighty, if we are strong," "under" the wrath of God, of toil, trouble, brevity, and sorrow (Ps. 90:7-10). Such theological/moral reckoning is counterbalanced by the force of diabological reflection. For Paul of Tarsus as a Jew of his time, death is to be numbered among the demonic powers that dominate the present age (I Cor. 15:24-25). The Devil has been widely apprehended, not alone as tempting to human sin, but as tied to death, even as the cause or agent of death. Sin and death become correlative. Sometimes Satan and Death are even equated.[18]

Many sophisticates of today characterize any case for the Devil as thoroughly anachronistic, an instance of leftover superstition. In apparent contrast, Ernest Becker maintains that it is the Devil who "reveals the reality of our situation, the fact that we can't really escape our earthly destiny." However, Becker reduces the Devil to an affair of scapegoating: "Somebody has to pay for the way things are"; this "is the meaning of the Devil in history.... The Devil represents the body, the absolute determinism of man's earthly condition.... To fight the Devil is to fight what he stands for...the negation of the spiritual victory over body-boundedness."[19]

The psychotherapist Rollo May is more objectivist, finding that "with *Moby Dick* [Herman] Melville joins the great writers of the middle and last half of the nineteenth century—Kierkegaard, Nietzsche, and several decades later Freud and Spengler. *All of them saw that the error of the Enlightenment was that it lacked a devil.*"[20] And Jeffrey Burton Russell points out that the crucial question any idea faces "is not whether it is outdated but whether it is true." Russell rightly equates superstition with beliefs that fail to fit into a coherent world view. This kind of failure in no way applies to the Devil. Russell adds: "No theodicy that does not take the Devil fully into consideration is likely to be persuasive."[21] Along this line of reasoning, we may even speak of the Devil as a kind of expert in theodicy; it is he who marshals the perfect justification for Evil: Himself.[22]

The attribution of death now to God and now to the Devil forces a grand and dread question: Who is in charge here? Sometimes any essential differentiation between the two sides is seen to break down; things divine and things diabolic come to converge. Thus, in application of Jungian thought, the Devil may be approached via the symbol Shadow of God.[23] Professor Russell calls attention to a decisive theological/moral paradox: "The study of the Devil indicates that historically, he is a manifestation of the divine, a part of the deity. *Sine diabolo nullus Deus.* Yet, morally, his work is completely and utterly to be rejected."[24] I number this paradox among the prevailing watchwords of the present book and indeed of my trilogy as a whole. Here is a place where a given secular historian (Jeffrey Burton Russell) expresses a wisdom not quite attained by a given New Testament theologian (Walter Wink). A straightforward translation of Russell would be: If we are ever going to reject radical evil we have to punish God as Devil; or, somewhat stronger: Unless we reject God, in God's culpability for radical evil and suffering, we ally ourselves with the Devil.

Russell's dialectical finding is not incoherent with Martin Luther's rendering of a *coincidentia oppositorum*: Wherever Jesus Christ is present, the Devil is present as well, yet wherever the Devil is at work, there arises Jesus Christ to thwart him.[25] We are also reminded of C. G. Jung's midrash upon the phrase in the Lord's Prayer, "Lead us not into temptation": "Is not this really the business of the *tempter,* the devil himself?"[26] In contrast to the Freudian persuasion that the Devil and God are no more than personifications of repressed, unconscious drives, Jung interprets them as omnipresent realities of the psyche as such. In elevating certain elements of the human unconscious to a collective unconscious, Jung sees these as transcending the individual psyche. Thus does the Devil reflect an autonomous, timeless, universal collective unconscious.[27]

IV

Several are the ways that human beings have tried to separate God from the Devil, that is to say, to save God from the attribution of radical evil, or at least of responsibility for that evil. One such major device is unqualified dualism, which relieves God of culpability by postulating an evil divine (diabolic) principle engaged in abiding conflict with God (as in Zoroastrianism). Opposite to this is the kind of radical monotheism that seeks to face the unending oppressiveness of evil by asserting the sovereign power of God, yet which, in making God responsible for all that happens, cannot escape associating evil with God (cf. Isa. 45:7: "I make weal and create woe"). The massive challenge to dualism is: What is to be the fate of goodness? And the terrible dilemma of monism is that radical evil stays rife.

The deficiencies of dualism and of monism can be offset, but only at a price: the admission of some kind of link between God and Devil, the path I myself take, with some hesitation and much sadness. Yet that link has its happier side. The persuasion that the Devil's work may be said somehow to precede evils committed by humanity—a viewpoint attested to in recent times by Reinhold Niebuhr[28]—counteracts in a positive, morally valuable way the travesty of making humankind, and not God, the subject of rebuke for the horrors of this world, including the specter of death. Niebuhr's protestation is echoed in Jung: If the Devil "fell away from God of his own free will" this helps establish "that evil was in the world before man, and therefore that man cannot be the sole author of it."[29]

It is as, so to speak, the Shadow of God—indeed as an instrument of God, God's (vocational) "fallen angel"[30]—that the Devil enters the cosmic/world stage. The classical tie of the Devil to Death thus gains a certain plausibility. Of course, this is not to exempt the human being from all moral liability. The biblical myth of the Fall, writes Niebuhr, "seeks to do justice to both the universality of sin and self-regard and to the element of personal responsibility in each sinful act."[31] In a word, humanity remains proximately blameworthy for evil, but never ultimately blameworthy.

To affirm the culpability of the Devil does not establish any innocence of God. It could do so only within the kind of radical dualism that fabricates the Devil as a sovereign Being wholly independent of God. Within the bounds of our Western religious tradition, culpability for all evil, including the final evil of death (the "last enemy"; I Cor. 15:26) has to be borne ultimately, if not proximately, by God. God is, so to speak, the first and final sinner.

Accordingly, such appellations of the Devil as Shadow of God and "fallen angel" help sustain two important economies: a denial of sovereignty to the Evil One (against the predicament of metaphysical/religious dualism) and at the same time a refusal to exculpate God from blameworthiness for evil (against the predicament of metaphysical/religious monism).

An ineluctable yet transparent warrant for the seemingly brazen charge of divine culpability and sinfulness is that no human being ever asked to be born (would it not be rather bizarre if they could do so?) or, in consequence, to be subjected to death, the final insult, the final evil vis-à-vis life. We humans are, with all organisms, the subjects/objects of *thrownness,* adjuncts of God's (ostensible) decision to make a world. In H. Richard Niebuhr's words, "we are 'thrown into existence,' fated to be.... [We] did not elect ourselves into being." This "self which lives in this body and this mind did not choose itself."[32] Erich Fromm observes that "we are cast into the world at a time and in a place we did not choose, and we are destined to leave that world...at a time and in a place that is not ours to choose."[33] And as Albert Camus has said, in words I find myself repeating in my late years, "Man is not entirely to blame; it is not he who started history."[34]

Is it not this thrownness that makes humanity into an essentially comic reality?

And is not God the responsible party?—once we assert that there *is* a God.

Many people have been indoctrinated with the notion that "the power to create is the power to destroy." Who says so? Since when does the ability to create bestow any automatic right to instill or permit terror? In essence, the human organism is, with other organisms, an innocent bystander who has been thrust into an infinity of events that is not of its substantive making. To endeavor to take the blame for evil away from God and to visit it upon humankind, through such ideological and politicizing constructions as "sin" and "free will," suggests a conspiracy that is integral to the Devil's special work. Who but the Devil himself could be that ingeniously immoral and unjust?

In Western thinking, God is said to be Lord and Defender of Life, contra Death. God is rightly petitioned to "deliver my life from the wicked" (Ps. 17:13). But all too often things fail to work out that way, while in the final reckoning (death) they fail completely. In addition, do not the wicked also have a right to live? Jesus of Nazareth declared (in the context of a resurrection-to-come) that God "is not of the dead but of the living" (Matt. 22:32). Unfortunately, even a resurrection from the dead spares no one the horror of death.

The *New Oxford Annotated Bible* is evidently trying to face up to the terror of death via its midrash, "those who are related to God in faith have life even though physically dead; resurrection is the divine act by which they will achieve the fullness of life intended in creation and lost through sin and death."[35] The reasoning here is troublesome in at least five respects, each one of ascending moral seriousness: What of those souls who are not related to God in faith? Why arrange a universe in which sin is allowed (allegedly) as an element decisive to death? Why use so horrible an evil as death as a door to fullness of life? What possible justification could there be for putting the innocents (e.g., little children), through the horror of death? And why ever sanction death in the first place? Questions such as these reveal the moral futility of, indeed the evil in, the counsel that one's coming death is quite acceptable and even fine, because after all overpopulation is a menace and someone else ought to be given the chance to live.[36] Indeed, various proposed theodicean answers to any or all of the five questions pale before the patriarch Abraham's impregnable query, "Shall not the Judge of all the earth do what is just?" (Gen. 18:25).

Norman Podhoretz states: "God wants us to live," whereas the Devil wants us to choose death. "Suicide is thus the supreme act of obeisance to the Devil."[37] Podhoretz's dichotomy is challenged by the truth that it is God who kills us off, or at a minimum does not prevent our being killed off. However, it is only the believer in God who is led, with the heaviest of hearts, to tender this judgment against God. When Abraham besought God ("Shall not the Judge of all the earth do what is just?"), he was hardly addressing Nature or some Blind Force. Humanists and atheists may rest content (if it does manage to content them) with the fact of human beings and/or natural forces as exclusive culprits for all the world's ills, including death. The question of evil, headed by the terror of death, is thus viewed quite differently within a religious outlook in contradistinction to a nonreligious outlook. The religious view takes the evil of death, indeed all evil, much more seriously than do humanist or atheist representations, since nothing could be more heartrending than being compelled to correlate existentially God and radical evil.

V

Is there, then, any road between and beyond the predicament of un-qualified dualism and the predicament of unqualified monism? If some creative people have succeeded in linking comedy to God-as-such (e.g., Dante Alighieri's *Commedia*; today Gerhard Staguhn's *God's Laughter*) and even to the Devil-as-such (e.g., William Langland's *Piers Plowman*; Arnoul Gréban's *Passion*), perhaps we may envision as well the pertinence of comedy, not merely to a God/Devil symbiosis but, much more significantly, to the drama of ultimate victory (should there ever be such) of good over evil. The adventure before us is: In what regard, if any, may comedy (human and/or divine) come to grips with radical evil, including the final evil of death?

Before we pursue the above haunting query, we must complete the foundations of this book with a word upon the quality and meaning of comedy and the comic vision.

Notes

1. Betty Friedan, *The Fountain of Age* (New York: Simon & Schuster, 1993).
2. Joan Rivers, in "Next Time, Dear God, Please Choose Someone Else: Jewish Humour—American Style," *Arena*, BBC Television, 23 February, 1990.
3. Julien Green, *God's Fool: The Life and Times of Francis of Assisi*, trans. Peter Heinegg (San Francisco: Harper & Row, 1985), 249.
4. Eric W. Gritsch, *Martin—God's Court Jester: Luther in Retrospect* (Philadelphia: Fortress Press, 1983), 6.
5. Wendy Farley, *Tragic Vision and Divine Compassion* (Louisville: Westminster/ John Knox Press, 1990), 37.
6. Nomothetic analysis concerns itself with generalizations; idiography deals with the individual, or with what we might deem the mystery of the single case.
7. Søren Kierkegaard, *Parables of Kierkegaard*, ed. Thomas C. Oden (Princeton: Princeton University Press, 1978), 30 (from *Stages on Life's Way*).
8. See Fred Setterberg, "Zora Neale Hurston in the Land of 1,000 Dances," *The Georgia Review* 46 (1992): 627–43.
9. Consult, for example, the analyses of this phenomenon in Mahadev L. Apte, "Sexual Inequality in Humor," in *Humor and Laughter: An Anthropological Approach* (Ithaca-London: Cornell University Press, 1985); Michael Mulkay, "Sexual Humour and Gender Relationships," in *On Humor: Its Nature and Its Place in Modern Society* (Cambridge: Basil Blackwell, 1988); and especially Nancy A. Walker, *A Very Serious Thing: Women's Humor and American Culture* (Minneapolis: University of Minnesota Press, 1988).
10. Mulkay, *On Humor*, 211.
11. G. Tom Milazzo, *The Protest and the Silence* (Minneapolis: Fortress Press, 1992), 24.

12. Thus, Milazzo concedes that the divine-human encounter itself "will always be deeply problematic" because the presence of the divine appears "to recede infinitely into the darkness...of hiddenness" (ibid.).

13. Ernest Becker, *Escape From Evil* (New York: Free Press, 1975), 1.

14. Ernest Becker, *The Denial of Death* (New York: Free Press, 1973), 11, 21, 57. It was William James who called death "the worm at the core" of human pretensions to happiness (*The Varieties of Religious Experience* [New York: Mentor Edition, 1958], 121). See also Norbert Elias, *The Loneliness of the Dying,* trans. Edmund Jephcott (Oxford: Basil Blackwell, 1985); Lloyd R. Bailey, Sr., *Biblical Perspectives on Death* (Philadelphia: Fortress Press, 1979); and A. Roy Eckardt, "Death in the Judaic and Christian Traditions," in Arien Mack, ed., *Death in American Experience* (New York: Schocken Books, 1973), 123–48.

15. Daphne Hampson, *Theology and Feminism* (Oxford: Basil Blackwell, 1990), 137–45.

16. *The New York Times* (26 August 1993).

17. Gerhard Staguhn, *God's Laughter: Man and His Cosmos,* trans. Steve Lake and Caroline Mähl (New York: HarperCollins, 1992), 105–06.

18. Jeffrey Burton Russell, *The Devil: Perceptions of Evil from Antiquity to Primitive Christianity* (Ithaca-London: Cornell University Press, 1987), 240; see also 216, 256; *Satan: The Early Christian Tradition* (Ithaca-London: Cornell University Press, 1987), 119; S. G. F. Brandon, *The Judgment of the Dead: The Idea of Life After Death in the Major Religions* (New York: Charles Scribner's Sons, 1967), 114. After the eleventh century, death and the Devil are usually portrayed separately (Jeffrey Burton Russell, *Lucifer: The Devil in the Middle Ages* [Ithaca-London: Cornell University Press, 1986], 210). As the Middle Ages wore on, a new and diabolic twinning was accentuated, the Devil and the Jews; on this development, see Joel Carmichael, *The Satanizing of the Jews* (New York: Fromm International, 1992), 54 ff.

19. Becker, *Escape From Evil,* 122–23.

20. Rollo May, *The Cry For Myth* (New York: W. W. Norton, 1991), 283 (italics in original).

21. Russell, *The Devil,* 228.

22. In *How To Tell God From the Devil* (New Brunswick-London: Transaction Publishers, Rutgers University, 1995), chap. 1 and *passim* (hereinafter HTT), and following Jeffrey Burton Russell, I provide a full exposition of the Devil as the personification of absolute evil. Cf. Walter Wink: "'Satan' is the actual power that congeals around collective idolatry, injustice, or inhumanity, a power that increases or decreases according to the degree of collective refusal to choose higher values" (*Naming the Powers* [Philadelphia: Fortress Press, 1984], 105). Yet Wink declares that he prefers "to think of the powers [which include Satan] as impersonal entities" (*Engaging the Powers* [Minneapolis: Fortress Press, 1992], 8; see also 57–59, 148). I construe the Devil as personal (and superpersonal).

23. Consult Jeffrey Burton Russell, *The Prince of Darkness: Radical Evil and the Power of Good in History* (Ithaca-London: Cornell University Press, 1992), 245–48; cf. C. G. Jung, "Good and Evil in Analytical Psychology," *Civilization in Transition, Collected Works* 10, trans. R. F. C. Hull (London: Routledge & Kegan Paul, 1964), 456–68. See also Jung, "The Shadow," *Collected Works* 9, trans. R. F. C. Hull (Princeton: Princeton University Press, 1968), 3–7; "The Light With the Shadow," *Collected Works* 10, 218–26.

24. Russell, *The Devil*, 31-32. Walter Wink appears to edge toward dualism when, in speaking of Satan as "master of this age," he makes "the total world-system...a conspiracy against God, a lie perpetuated by people and presided over by Satan" (*Naming the Powers*, 83). It is valid to identify the Devil in terms of a conspiracy against God's own righteousness, but it is invalid to locate the conspiracy "outside" or "beyond" God. If the Devil may be said to be in rebellion against God (ibid., 84), we yet have to insist that in some positive sense, divine self-rebellion is involved. Jeffrey Burton Russell speaks of the Devil as the personification of evil; Wink maintains that "personification is too rationalistic to deal with" such an archetypal reality as Satan (*Unmasking the Powers* [Philadelphia: Fortress Press, 1986], 24-25).

25. See Heiko A. Oberman, *Luther: Man between God and the Devil*, trans. Eileen Welliser-Schwarzbart (New York: Doubleday, 1992), 156.

26. C. G. Jung, *The Archetypes and the Collective Unconscious, Collected Works* 9, I, trans. R. F. C. Hull (London: Routledge & Kegan Paul, 1959), 214. The NRSV substitutes "do not bring us to the time of trial" (Matt. 6:13).

27. Consult Russell, *Prince of Darkness*, 242-48. A Jungian analyst, June Singer, describes the collective unconscious "as an extension of the personal unconscious to its wider and broader base, encompassing contents" held in common by the family, social group, tribe and nation, race, and eventually all humanity. "The wonder of the collective unconscious is that it is all these, all the legend and history of the human race, with its demons and its gentle saints, its mysteries and its wisdom, all within each of us—a microcosm within the macrocosm" (*Boundaries of the Soul* [Garden City: Doubleday Anchor Books, 1977], 95-96).

28. Consult Reinhold Niebuhr, *The Nature and Destiny of Man* I (New York: Charles Scribner's Sons, 1941), 180-81, 254. Niebuhr's exposition of the Devil and the issue of ultimate responsibility for moral evil is fully analyzed in my HTT, chap. 6. See in this connection Bernhard W. Anderson, *Creation versus Chaos: The Reinterpretation of Mythical Symbolism in the Bible* (Philadelphia: Fortress Press, 1987), 164-70; more generally, chap. 5, "Creation and Conflict." Walter Wink writes: If the "first fall" is that of humankind, "the second fall is that of the angels: there is a rupture in the very spirituality of the universe (Gen. 6:1-4). *Human sin cannot therefore account for all evil*" (*Engaging the Powers* [Minneapolis: Fortress Press, 1992], 77, my italics).

29. C. G. Jung, *Aion: Researches into the Phenomenology of the Self, Collected Works* 9, II, trans. R. F. C. Hull (London: Routledge & Kegan Paul, 1959), 48.

30. See Russell, *The Devil*, 227-28, 241-43, 252-53. Cf. Job 1:6 ff.; Eph. 2:1-2; Rev. 12:7-9. Consult also Geddes MacGregor, "Satan: The Realm of Angels Gone Wrong," in *Angels: Ministers of Grace* (New York: Paragon House, 1988).

31. Reinhold Niebuhr, *The Self and the Dramas of History* (New York: Charles Scribner's Sons, 1955), 99.

32. H. Richard Niebuhr, *Faith on Earth: An Inquiry into the Structure of Human Faith*, ed. Richard R. Niebuhr (New Haven-London: Yale University Press, 1989), 65.

33. Erich Fromm, *The Anatomy of Human Destructiveness* (New York: Holt, Rinehart and Winston, 1973), 225. The second part of Fromm's assertion has to be qualified; many people do exert influence upon the event of their death, e.g., chronic tobacco users. Again, the suicide determines, or at least has a part in, the time and place of death.

34. Albert Camus, *The Rebel* (New York: Vintage, 1956), 297.
35. *The New Oxford Annotated Bible, New Revised Standard Version* (New York: Oxford University Press, 1991), commentary on Matt. 22:31-32.
36. Employing statistical techniques, J. Richard Gott III, a Princeton University physicist, predicts that intelligent human beings may endure on Earth a maximum of 7.8 million years (though a minimum of 5,128 years from now) (*The New York Times,* 1 June 1993). Any such prediction—even the minimal one—brings no consolation whatsoever to the individual of today. Another physicist, Eric J. Lerner, condemns Gott's form of futurism, charging him with engaging in pseudo-statistics and pseudo-science ("Horoscopes for Humanity," *The New York Times,* OP-ED page, 14 July 1993). As we might anticipate, Gott then accuses Lerner of misreading his paper (letter to *The New York Times,* 27 July 1993). Query: Must scientists disagree as much as, or more than, religionists?
37. Norman Podhoretz, "Speak of the Devil, *Commentary* 51 (April 1971): 6. Cf. John B. Cobb, Jr., "The Right to Die," in *Matters of Life and Death* (Louisville: Westminster/John Knox Press, 1991).

2

A Word for Comic Vision

Humor isn't pretty.
—Steve Martin

We come more intensively to the question of possible meanings of "comedy" and "humor" together with their differentiation. I am not unaware of the wry reaction that the attempt to define humor may itself be "one of the definitions of humor."[1] For S. J. Perelman, "any exegesis of humor is both fatal and dull." Since I am not knowingly a masochist, I guess I think Perelman goes a bit too far.

A favorite line of Sam Goldwyn was, "Before I begin, I'd like to say something." The something I'd like to say before I begin consists of an important caveat: It is a serious blunder to reduce comedy to something that is funny. Much comedy (incongruity) is anything but funny. The foremost case of this is death. At the same time, I do not mean to make funniness and death totally exclusive of each other. A scenario of Adolf Hitler and some of his cohorts caught inside, rather than remaining outside, one of their own gas chambers, death pits, or crematoria comes deliciously to mind.[2]

Now I shall begin. I offer ten assertions. Sometimes I tend to think decalogically.

1. Ralph C. Wood is not being careless when he uses "comedy" and "humor" and even "laughter" interchangeably.[3] Such a procedure affords a certain flexibility to the work of the interpreter, helping him or her to: (a) vary usage depending upon the demands and exigencies of context, and (b) live with the fact that there are infinite usages of "comedy," infinite usages of "humor," and a whole congeries of analyses of

their relation. Throughout the book we shall exemplify this variety. To say that comedy is this and only this is like trying to say that religion or science or art is this and only this.[4]

2. A formidable methodological complication is the ambiguous, multiflavored quality that comprises the objective realm of comedy. Thus, the life of comedy can range all the way from a certain orientation within writing, speaking, and performing; to a theatrical/dramatic enterprise; to the issue of what is right and what is wrong (cf. below, Elayne Boosler's linkage of humor and justice); to a reflection of misery (cf. Joan Rivers, cited toward the beginning of chapter 1); to an ontological dimension;[5] to affirmations respecting religious faith (the "divine comedy")—and, for that matter, to comic devilishness.

In accordance with the vastness of the phenomenon before us, Marcel Gutwirth can, in his "essay on the comic," reach a fivefold conclusion: (a) Laughter is an intellectual emotion. Involved here are interpreters who center their attention upon the category of incongruity (Kant, Hegel, Schopenhauer, Bergson), as well as those who concentrate upon elation, high spirits, euphoria, joy, the spontaneity of childhood, and the spirit of play; (b) Comic laughter entails an element of surprise, which involves in turn unexpectedness and/or instantaneity, and which in either case "compresses into a single moment the risible contradiction"; (c) "Aristotle's painless deformity combines with Hobbes's sudden glory to situate the comic in the realm of an inconsequential violence, a painless aggression." Hence, "what Hobbes and in their turn Bossuet, Baudelaire, Lamennais, and the rest mistake for the essence of laughter, the self's peak of victory over others, may be no more than the condition for laughter: a self utterly secure, for the nonce"; (d) In a large number of ways, laughter spells freedom—on the one hand, "a discharge of aggressive energy" but with "so little harm done"; on the other hand, freedom *from*, or liberation. (Perhaps we may comment that while tragedy bespeaks fate [*moira*], comedy embodies, or at least covets, hopefulness and an open future.); (e) There is the all-encompassing feature of reversal. "Reaching all the way back to Kant's expectation reduced to nothing and, by way of [Alexander] Bain's degradation of an object possessing dignity, all the way forward to the irrealist's view that reality itself is for a moment thrown into doubt, a scenario unfolds before our eyes of the brief victory of the lesser over the greater, the worse over the better, the no-account over the weighty." Thus is the mind's higher function (connecting data, drawing out a pattern, finding a meaning) "tripped up on the failure to exercise the lower one, simple recognition of the obvious. It picks itself up, smiling.... 'Nothing' ceases to be mere absence, it climbs into the bosom of Being, nestles there as if by rights, and in a spirit of mild reproof worthy of Montaigne settles down for good in the realm that spurns it."[6]

3. Marie Collins Swabey, among many others including myself, ties comedy to the incongruous and the ludicrous (cf. Gutwirth's initial category). "The most adequate generic definition of the comic is: the presence of an incongruity, contradiction, or absurdity that is humanly relevant without being oppressively grave or momentous. It is in this strictest sense that we use the word as a synonym for the ludicrous."[7] John Morreall goes so far as to propose that "the essence of humor lies in the enjoyment of incongruity, even ultimate incongruity."[8] Peter L. Berger puts it nicely: "The essence of the comic is discrepancy."[9] Comedy entails a split, a cleft, a breaking asunder.

4. There are grounds for linking comedy to *myth,* the latter of which is an oft-used hermeneutical instrument for relating transcendent reality and the immanent world around us.[10] Myth works to clear a path between two mysteries, the mystery of ultimate fact (Nature? God?) and the mystery of human interpretive wisdom,[11] a way between ostensibly objective data and subjective creativity and invention. Myth ventures upon "truths" and "claims" that, in phrasing from Reinhold Niebuhr, are to be taken "seriously though not literally."[12] Comedy and humor seek after a comparable mediating role between ultimate fact and human imagination, thereby contributing to fresh mysteries though, ideally, no less impressive ones, perchance even joyous ones.

5. We noted in chapter 1 Søren Kierkegaard's tie between "the comic" (caricature) and suffering. It is possible to give honor to comedy/humor as a brigade massed in a battle with death—no hope of victory, of course, but yet one way to "go down" (that is, to move from "earth" to "heaven"?) that just may rival, or at least complement, other ways. From this perspective, one reason that comedy/humor *as an opportunity* may be taken much more seriously than tragedy is that in the depths of tragedy human choice and freedom end up obliterated. What could inevitability ever do to *deserve* celebration or even special attention? Tragedy bespeaks fate, entrapment, death. My own inclination is to connect comedy with spontaneity and creativity: inchoately, this kitten and small

child scrambling all over the place; more sophisticatedly, the ecstasy of human love, God forgiving the sinner, even the human being forgiving God—all in all, an exaltation of life (let the sureties of death be damned). On this reading, comedy is perhaps perceivable as a relatively larger category than humor as such, verging even upon the ontic sublimity of freedom itself (self- and world-transcendence), whereas humor may be a little more subjective and a little more fleeting. Comedy points toward the possibility of redemption of some kind (tragedy to its lack).

6. Any associating of comedy with freedom (cf. Gutwirth's fourth category) must be on the watch against at least two pitfalls, well delineated by Ralph C. Wood. Professor Wood distinguishes among comedy as "sheer vitalistic energy," comedy as "covert nihilism," and "the comedy of redemption." As I interpret or at least apply Wood's reasoning, the potential fault lies in reducing or accommodating the third of these to either or both the first two.

On the one hand and firstly, "much of human jubilation arises from mere animal high spirits.... Comic licentiousness and exuberance are suspect because they implicitly deny that there is any reality beyond earthly reality." Wood goes so far as to adjudge that "comic art and ritual immerse their celebrants in the heedless flux of natural life." At this level, comedy thus aims "to allay and assuage the vagaries of fortune, fending off calamity by means of laughter." My response to the last sentence, if only from a gathering geriatric perspective, is to wonder what is wrong with this "fending off," although Wood quickly and helpfully continues that comic laughter also has the positive purpose of celebrating "human adroitness and ingenuity in recovering our lost equilibrium." However, he equally insists that our "animal exuberance" only serves to mock "the moral principles that preserve society" against uncontrolled passion, and he implies agreement with Susanne Langer that comedy, at least at this first level, tends to trivialize the human struggle for purpose and meaning.[13]

I would add that once the liberational door to the world of comedy is opened, it is very difficult and perhaps even unwise to rule out and/or repress things bodily, including the violent, the erotic, the scatological. Comedy deprived of these elements descends from freedom into restrictiveness. Human freedom itself is never safe from the danger of slavery.

On the other hand and secondly, comedy can be covertly nihilistic, whereby it bends "back upon itself in moral self-criticism and irony."

This eventuality is manifest in the so-called black humorists: "Humanity awakens from its slumbering animality only to confront cosmic nothingness: the blankness and emptiness of the unanswering heavens.... [The] black humorist breaks into bitter peals of laughter. This darker kind of comedy sees no way of reconciling the human cry for meaning with the ultimate meaninglessness of the cosmos. Humanity's self-transcending freedom is not something admirable and salutary...but a bad joke at best and a horrid mistake at worst." Even more terribly than tragedy, comedy in this second form threatens "to fling us into a vortex that dissolves all distinctions, into an infinite regress of mockery mocking the mocker, until every thing becomes equally ridiculous and life is reduced to a madhouse of mirrors. The comic paradoxes nihilistically multiply, until we are finally brought around to the banal truism that we laugh in order not to weep."[14]

7. Wood argues that the divine comedy of redemption escapes the two pitfalls just described. For the present, and in some alliance with Wood, I might make reference to a potential remedy that endeavors to link comedy/humor with truth and morality—a possibility not inconsonant with Wood's own variation upon the comic vision. At this juncture, I return to argumentation in my *Sitting in the Earth and Laughing*.

In *Comic Laughter,* Marie Collins Swabey maintains that "in the laughter of comic insight we achieve a logical moment of truth; while metaphysically, through some darting thought, we detect an incongruence as canceled by an underlying congruence. We gain an inkling, as it were, of the hang of things, sometimes even a hint of cosmic beneficence. [In the little incredible kitten and puppy, is not God trying to *break through*?—A.R.E.] In short, perception of the ludicrous helps us to comprehend both ourselves and the world, making us, at least in the highest reaches of humor, feel more at home in the universe by aiding in the discernment of values."

By exposing fallacies in thought, language, and ways of living, minds alert to the ludicrous may contribute not a little to human progress.... By uncovering neglected hypocrisies, illusions, vanities, and deceptions in the behavior of persons and societies [I should include here the highly dubious behavior of God.—A.R.E], avoidance of error is promoted as well as knowledge of the truth. Neat presentations by the humorist of instances of men's vain conceit of their appearance, wealth, or wisdom, their pretensions to be what they are not, their illusions of grandeur, good looks, sagacity...remove in part our blindness with regard to certain factual and moral weaknesses in mankind. Similarly the sudden grasp of cases of contradiction between word and deed, of men not practicing what they preach, of talking one way and acting another, in tickling our sense of the ludicrous may enlighten us as to sources of wrongdoing in ourselves and others.[15]

(Query: In keeping with my interjection within the above passage, is it not possible to apply this critical moral function of comic laughter respecting the human condition to the divine condition as well? If not, why not? We noted in chapter 1 Abraham's audacious address to God: "Shall not the Judge of all the earth do what is just?")

Swabey continues: To the critic who asks why comics cannot be wholly freed "from moral and rational canons," the answer is that "a completely hodge-podge world would have no discriminable qualities or meanings sufficient to denote the comic." Stated in other terms, there is no way to play the game that is, *in essentia,* comic laughter without the presence of rules. "Because reason is universal and thinking operates through the universal, the comic cannot be freed from moral categories.... In the long run the logic of a realm in which vice is treated like virtue, inhumanity like humanity, the fiendish like the friendly, the decent like the depraved must finally, by evading all responsibility to law and order, drown itself in a chaos of nonsense."[16]

I might venture a comment upon the domain of nonsense as alluded to by Swabey. I happen to be a lover of nonsense. In chapter 4 I will utilize, in a theological frame of reference, the instrument of nonsense as one variation upon humor, but I do not think that this will mean ultimate disagreement with Swabey.[17] She rightly speaks of "*pure nonsense* as signifying utter meaninglessness or absence of rationality," and hence not funny. But I believe that there can be sense in nonsense (as also nonsense in sense). As I put the matter in *Sitting in the Earth,* nonsense need not be equated with senselessness. Nonsense "does not have to be ridiculous." It can make "much moral and intellectual sense. Since good nonsense is highly clever, there is no way to cut it off from the life of the mind. We may remember that Sigmund Freud finds nonsense not merely enjoyable but also reasonable; it permits us 'to withdraw from the pressure of critical reason.' Morton Gurewitch supports Freud in the contention that it is necessary periodically to abandon and dismantle reason and reality. I would simply add that such negation in and through nonsense is not possible without serious intellectual exertion."[18]

I think here of the celebrated work of Edward Lear.[19] In the measure that human beings more or less inevitably fall into idolatry, Edward

Lear is an idol of mine. But I am given to understand that Lear is also a special idol of God Godself, so I plead forgiveness on the ground of *imitatio dei*. (Nagging query: Can God have idols? Come to think of it, idolatry-by-the-divine would bring incalculable relief to us, probably assuring a kind of redemption, and causing the angels to laugh. My own private/public idol is my wife. What if she is as well God's idol? Best idea I ever had! Up with idolatry, down with "high religion"!)

We may conclude the case for the morality and truth of comedy with the aid of findings from two skilled comedians of today. "Real comedy can't be learned; it comes from a need for justice" (Elayne Boosler). "The funniest joke of all is the absolute truth stated simply and gracefully" (Carl Reiner).[20] Comic vision is, from this perspective, 20/20 vision.

8. Perhaps the phrase I just used, "comic vision," does as well as any to epitomize our advocated world of comedy/humor/laughter.[21] Such, at least, is the reasoning behind my subtitle, *Essays Toward a Comic Vision.*

9. Perhaps most important of all, I tend to think of comedy/ humor in functional terms as a weapon—if one of highly limited power—against the evils of *repression*. The most formidable act of repression is the repression of Death. Accordingly, if I appear in the pages to come to be taking undue or strange liberties in what I have to say about God and the divine ways, I hope you will continue to keep in mind this particular vocation I have, wrongly or wisely, chosen for comedy. I hope you will not think of me as perforce unregenerate or irreverent. I yearn, before I die, to *break out* if I can: to break out of *show,* to break into *honesty.*

10. Apart from my allusion to Gutwirth's representation, I have not referred to laughter in and for itself, as I view it. No disquisition is needed. Laughter is simply comedy/humor gone out marching in a parade for all to see—among humans and even some other animals, a physiological exercise.[22] (Query: Is the laughter of God in any sense physiological? See chapter 4.)

All in all, human comedy is a powerful, pulsating, immense corpus. It expands out into the abiding universal of incongruity; it contracts into the fleeting particular of a chuckle. In between live a thousand nuances: mischief and ineptitude,[23] defiance and acceptance, prophetism and re-action, the forgiving and the sardonic, verbal tricks and pantomime, scatology and eschatology, tomfoolery and satire, cartoons and prat-falls, joy and resignation, and the list goes on. For me, comedy, preeminently, opens the path to joy, even though it may not always be joyful in itself and cannot, tragically, ever guarantee joy.

With the above broad/deep apprehension of comedy/humor/laughter before us, we may ready ourselves for a practical confrontation with incongruity and absurdity but, more than that, for adventures with freedom and joy—perhaps catching sight along the way of a few signs of human liberation and even redemption. In sum, I am not quite ready to classify this book (or my trilogy in its entirety) as a work of fiction, though of course it is not nonfiction. It is... well, let's see what it is, or what it is trying to be.

Notes

1. An anonymous source cited in Henry Eilbirt, *What Is a Jewish Joke? An Excursion into Jewish Humor* (Northvale, N.J.-London: Jason Aronson, 1993), 1.
2. Consult Steve Lipman, *Laughter In Hell: The Use of Humor during the Holocaust* (Northvale, N.J.-London: Jason Aronson, 1991).
3. Ralph C. Wood, *The Comedy of Redemption: Christian Faith and Comic Vision in Four American Novelists* (Notre Dame: University of Notre Dame Press, 1988), 4 and *passim*. In his famous essay "Humour and Faith," Reinhold Niebuhr never uses the word *comedy*—though he is certainly concerned with comedy—and he never distinguishes between *humor* and *laughter* (*Discerning the Signs of the Times* [New York: Charles Scribner's Sons, 1946], 111–31). Marcel Gutwirth is not afraid to interweave laughter and comedy: *Laughing Matter: An Essay on the Comic* (Ithaca-London: Cornell University Press, 1993).
4. On the general subject of comedy/humor, consult, among many relevant works, George Aichele, Jr., *Theology as Comedy: Critical and Theoretical Implications* (Lanham, Md.: University Press of America, 1980); Mahadev Apte, *Humor and Laughter: An Anthropological Approach* (Ithaca, N.Y.: Cornell University Press, 1985); A. J. Chapman and H. C. Foot, eds., *It's a Funny Thing, Humour* (Oxford: Pergamon Press, 1977); Sarah Blacher Cohen, ed., *Comic Relief: Humor in Contemporary American Literature* (Urbana: University of Illinois Press, 1978); Christie Davies, *Ethnic Humor Around the World: A Comparative Analysis* (Bloomington: Indiana University Press, 1990); J. Durant and C. J. Miller, eds., *Laughing Matters: A Serious Look at Humor* (New York: John Wiley, 1988); A. Roy Eckardt, *Sitting in the Earth and Laughing: A Handbook of Humor* (New Brunswick and London: Transaction Publishers, Rutgers University, 1992); Edward L. Galligan, *The Comic Vision in Literature* (Athens: The University of Georgia Press, 1984); Morton Gurewitch, *Comedy: The Irrational Vision* (Ithaca: Cornell University Press, 1975); Gutwirth, *Laughing Matter*; Robin Andrew Haig, *The Anatomy of Humor: Biopsychological and Therapeutic Perspectives* (Springfield Ill.: Charles Thomas, 1988); Norman N. Holland, *Laughter: A Psychology of Humor* (Ithaca, N.Y.: Cornell University Press, 1982; which includes a bibliography of theories of humor); *Humor: International Journal of Humor Research*, special number on "Current Issues in Psychological Humor Research," 6 (1993); Candace Lang, *Irony/Humor: Critical Paradigms* (Baltimore, Md.: Johns Hopkins

University Press, 1988); Susanne K. Langer, *Feeling and Form: A Theory of Art Developed from "Philosophy in a New Key"* (New York: Charles Scribner's Sons, 1953); Harry Levin, *Playboys and Killjoys: An Essay on the Theory and Practice of Comedy* (New York: Oxford University Press, 1987); John L'Heureux, *Comedians* (New York: Viking Penguin, 1990); John Morreall, ed., *The Philosophy of Laughter and Humor* (Albany: State University of New York Press, 1987); Morreall, *Taking Laughter Seriously* (Albany: State University of New York Press, 1983); Lance Olsen, *Circus of the Mind in Motion: Postmodernism and the Comic Vision* (Detroit: Wayne State University Press, 1990); Robert M. Polhemus, *Comic Faith: The Great Tradition From Austin to Joyce* (Chicago: University of Chicago Press, 1981); Roy Russell, *Life, Mind, and Laughter* (Chicago: Adams, 1987); Marie Collins Swabey, *Comic Laughter: A Philosophical Essay* (Hamden, Conn.: Archon Books, 1970); Nancy Walker, *A Very Serious Thing: Women's Humor and American Culture* (Minneapolis: University of Minnesota Press; and Wood, *The Comedy of Redemption*.

5. This orientation is typified in Swabey, *Comic Laughter.*
6. Gutwirth, *Laughing Matter,* 100–15.
7. Swabey, *Comic Laughter,* 28. Incongruity is of course treatable as well from the standpoints of tragedy-as-such and of irony-as-such, which in turn are not wholly separable from comedy.
8. Morreall, *Taking Laughter Seriously,* 47. On the history of theories of humor, consult Morreall, ed., *Philosophy of Laughter and Humor.*
9. Peter L. Berger, "Christian Faith and the Social Comedy," in Conrad Hyers, ed., *Holy Laughter: Essays on Religion in the Comic Perspective* (New York: Seabury Press, 1969), 123. This is not to say that the discrepant is *necessarily* comical.
10. This fourth item is adapted from chap. 1 of my *How To Tell God From the Devil* (New Brunswick and London: Transaction Publishers, Rutgers University, 1995). Cf. Rollo May's psychological/psychotherapeutic study, *The Cry for Myth* (New York: W. W. Norton, 1991).
11. Cf. Gutwirth, "Cosmic Wisdom," *Laughing Matter.*
12. Reinhold Niebuhr distinguishes between "permanent myths" and "pre-scientific myths," though himself preferring the concept "symbol" as escaping the skeptical connotation he finds in "myth." He defines permanent myths as those that "describe some meaning or reality, which is not subject to exact analysis but can nevertheless be verified in experience" (*The Self and the Dramas of History* [New York: Charles Scribner's Sons, 1955], 97). See also André Maurois, *Illusions* (New York and London: Columbia University Press, 1968). For Walter Wink myth, in the best sense, is "the privileged narrative by which a community has come to understand and relate to what it holds to be the ultimate meaning of reality" (*Unmasking the Powers* [Philadelphia: Fortress Press, 1986], 174).
13. Wood, *Comedy of Redemption,* 23–27.
14. Ibid., 28, 30.
15. Swabey, *Comic Laughter,* v, 11. Swabey's "logical moment of truth" points to potential linkages between comedy and rationality. Consult Robert Nozick, *The Nature of Rationality* (Princeton: Princeton University Press, 1993).
16. Swabey, *Comic Laughter,* 21, 22, 23; Eckardt, *Sitting in the Earth,* 50–51.
17. Cf. the following judgment, for which, unfortunately, I cannot find the source, although it sounds like my late friend Uriel Tal: "Nonsense is always nonsense, but the history of nonsense is scholarship."

18. Eckardt, *Sitting in the Earth*, 51; Swabey, *Comic Laughter*, 16; Sigmund Freud, *Jokes and Their Relation to the Unconscious*, trans. James Strachey (New York: W. W. Norton, 1960), 126; Gurewitch, *Comedy*, 112.

19. Edward Lear, *The Nonsense Books of Edward Lear* (New York: New American Library, 1964).

20. As cited in Eckardt, *Sitting in the Earth*, 206, 53.

21. Cf. Galligan, *Comic Vision*; Maria Harris, "Religious Educators and the Comic Vision," *Religious Education* 75 (1980): 422-32; Wood, *Comedy of Redemption*.

22. Cf. Marcel Gutwirth, *Laughing Matter*, 8-14 and *passim*. Gutwirth's chap. 1, "Laughter and Its Explicators," addresses the why of laughter. His chap. 5, "Laughter's Inner Springs: The Psychological Approach," reckons with the motivation of laughter. Respecting play vis-à-vis humor, Gutwirth writes that play "takes make-believe seriously, for the time being," while humor "takes reality playfully" (82). For Ralph C. Wood, the transmutation from laughter into comic vision is to be identified as "artistic" (*Comedy of Redemption*, 23).

23. Gutwirth, *Laughing Matter*, 52.

Part II

Pages from the Life Journey of God: The Middle One or Two Years

Storytellers tell their story as if their hearers were about to start off on a journey.... What storytelling reminds us of, virtuously, is that there is no dissociation between innerness and the outside world, between life and meaning: that is precisely the "moral of the story."

—Fernando Savater

3

Poor God

Biography, in its purer form...may be held the fairest meed of human virtue—one given and received in entire disinterestedness—since neither can the biographer hope for acknowledgment from the subject, nor the subject at all avail himself of the biographical distinction conferred.
—Herman Melville

I raise without delay the question evoked by the title of part II of this book: How could it ever be possible to tell the story—or even *a* story—of God? After all, God is God, and human beings are human beings. On the other hand, while a horse is a horse, and a human is a human, we can readily provide much of the life story of a horse (or, for that matter, of a tree or even of a building, though not their inner story). In the case of a horse we may observe the ongoing behavior and fortunes of the poor creature. Yet there is no way to observe directly, or even obliquely, the behavior of God—on the assumption that God does "behave."

I

I just referred to the horse as a "poor creature." I have an odd habit of using the word "poor" whenever I speak of the animals. I may have picked this up from my parents, both of whom would often speak this way. They shared a great sympathy for so-called dumb creatures. In any event, I myself sometimes feel sorry for the animals. (But not always; I can go for days without paying much attention to them, although sometimes I end up a little ashamed of myself for that. I ought not forget that every animal is a companion with me, and I am a companion with every

35

animal, in our shared destination of death. We are traveling together on the one train. We humans are, of course, no more than a special form of animal. Sometimes I find myself feeling sorry for all living/dying things—why, I don't really know. A psychiatrist might wish to orient me to a realization that I am no more than feeling sorry for myself.)

One reason I *think* I feel especially sorry for the animals—I must not exclude the birds, the fishes, every other creature—is that they do not seem to be able to say or know or appreciate who they are or what they are doing here. In *Platero y Yo,* Juan Ramón Jiménez tells his donkey, "Your eyes, which you do not see, Platero, and which you raise humbly to the sky, are two beautiful roses."[1] I find it sad that Platero must remain oblivious to his beauty. As I once wrote: "[T]he lot of the animals is not a tragic one, for tragedy entails accountability. The animals' plight is one of pathos. The heart of this pathos is the absence of comprehension. [This is in no way to insinuate that the 'higher animals' cannot think.[2]] Thus, the beauty of the animals within this world that frames their portrait remains a beauty they themselves can never know."[3]

Again, while human beings can and do assign names to animals, the animal cannot "know" its name in the way that we can know ours.[4] And further, when we speak to the animals (a persisting impulse), they do not seem capable of answering us in any I-thou way. In a word, the animals appear unable to enter into and to tell their own story. Is not all of this? (That humankind could ever "domesticate" a number of animal species appears quite out of the question. Happily, the impossible does happen.)

What we can at least do with the animals and birds and fish is to tell them that they are very beautiful and very good, and that we love them very much. They may only seldom hear us but at least we will have *assured* them, and that's something—a grand act of reprisal against the monster Death.

II

It strikes me that in some respects God may live in a plight not wholly dissimilar to that of the animals. For one thing, it may well be that God can use some assurance from us. For another thing, God and the animals would appear to take themselves rather seriously. (Later, we shall see how God may actually succeed in breaking out of that condition.)

"Karl Lorenz has a striking phrase, *tierischer Ernst* (animal earnest-ness), to convey our sense of the relentless in-dead-earnest that the ne-cessity to feed and propagate and survive against great odds, preyed upon and preying, enforces on the animal kingdom."[5] I have an idea that there is a comparable *göttlich Ernst,* brought on by, among other things, having to do daily battle with the Shadow.[6] Perhaps we can do something to help God lighten up a little.

Again, at least from our point of view—what other do we have?—God does not appear capable of narrating the divine story, at least not without some kind of help. It is fantastic to say it, yet it has to be said: God is dumb as the animals are dumb, as meanwhile we humans go around jabbering all over the place and filling the airways and libraries to overflowing. Clearly, this does not mean that the animals, fishes, and birds cannot communicate with one another. They do this all the time. Yet the idea of language seems to remain uniquely ours. In the same connection, a tradition of "the Word of God" abides, but it is difficult to subsume that category under empirical language. Besides, I am advised that God has produced relatively few books.

God would appear to be isolated from us, as perhaps from other lev-els of reality. Is that not sad? Yet how in the world are we ever to "get to" God, or at least get near enough to God to be able to represent God's story?—not, to be sure, as faithfully as God would wish it told, but at least as human beings may be called upon to tell it.

Sometimes I feel sorry for God (*daath elohim*)—not just because of God's Devil problem, but also because God may well get lonely.

I hope that this compassion for God is honest. In this connection I see that in E. M. Schorb's poem "Destruction," a little boy who has just been through the terror of a hurricane nevertheless says

> amazingly
> that he felt sorry
> for the wind.[7]

Are we to stop feeling sorry for God just because, as all too often seems the case, God is being destructive?

Having intimated that we just may be blocked from composing any life story of God, I conjecture that a potential way out—this is wild—might be to go the other way 'round. That is to say, instead of moving "up" frontally to God, we might move "down" to the animals—not necessarily excluding ourselves as animals—and only then turn back "up" to God.

Here is a working hypothesis (ratio and proportion, theological style): We are, so to speak, gods to the "lower" creation, particularly to our near sisters and brothers the animals, as God may be God to us.

Such an upside-down procedure as this could hardly ever furnish a rationale for all aspects of a story of God. Furthermore, my hypothesis cannot be unqualified, for the simple reason that the animals are innocent, that is, they lack freedom and responsibility (as far as we can tell), whereas the innocence of God (if that term is applicable) does not entail the absence of freedom and potential blameworthiness. On the other hand, the approach suggested might at least have the virtue of getting us started. It may help orient us, for purposes of the book. It may prompt some creative imaginings, or at a minimum some tantalizing speculation.

Here are a few potential parallels.

1. The creation account of Genesis has God saying, "Let us make humankind in our image, according to our likeness; and let them have dominion over the fish of the sea, and over the birds of the air, and over the cattle, and over all the wild animals of the earth, and over every creeping thing that creeps upon the earth" (Gen. 1:26; cf. Ps. 8:6-8). The tradition of *imago dei* establishes the dignity of humankind as a peculiar creature of God, or at least as a being in whom a singular relation between the divine and that dimension within creation called the human is made possible. And, in this regard, humankind is *assigned* the task of taking care of the animal and other creation. Human beings are created to be responsible surrogates amidst God's presumed, ultimate stewardship over the earth.

Application (Dream?): God is particularly responsible for taking care of humankind, which is, ostensibly, made in the divine image itself.

2. By implication, humankind is to be held accountable when it fails to meet its obligations to the animal world and to its environment as a whole.

Application (Dream?): God is to be held accountable when or if God fails to take care of humankind. Thus may God be legitimately put on trial should God be guilty of the crime of excessive human suffering, a condition for which human beings themselves could not possibly be blamed.

3. By the same implication as under point two, humankind merits a certain degree of praise when and if it lives up to its task of the stewardship of things earthly.

Application (Dream?): God is to be praised when and if God acts as God can and ought to behave (God as stepping out from behind the Shadow of radical evil). We ought to love the world, the creation; God ought to love us. The animals did not ask to be born; accordingly, it is well (valorous) for us to face up to that fateful situation in their behalf, simply by looking after them more than we have been doing. But neither did *we* ever ask to be born; God ought to face up, in our behalf, to that determining state of affairs. In point of fact, God is much more responsible for us than we are for animal and other life: The whole shooting match belongs to God. Yet what a job it all is for God. Poor God! (Did God ask to be God? Is God aware that God is beautiful? Does God secretly have and enjoy a name?[8] Yet is God able fully to appreciate who God is? Perhaps we small earthlings can be of a little aid to God here. But does God particularly care if or when we feel sorry for God? Yet may not God's own inner condition be one of pathos, in need of consolation, in need of love? Well, at least God does not have to die. Or is there something wrong with this last statement? In any case, I still think God can do with a bit more comedy and laughter.)

I seem to have fabricated for myself, as perhaps for you, a moral oxymoron: We are to be sorry for God; yet God had better behave Godself. (Not unlike the plight of human mother and father vis-à-vis child.)

III

To be sure, the way to God that I am musing upon here is hardly a strictly cognitive one of the sort we utilize in logical and scientific endeavor. It is an analogical way, subject to all the limitations of analogy. However, G. Tom Milazzo is overly skeptical in adjudging that analogical language about God "has no referent," since it has, allegedly, separated God "from the world."[9] I submit that only a theology of total negation would have that consequence: God is not at all this, God is not at all that. With the instrument of analogy, by contrast, there is provision for "like" and "unlike": God is like this beautiful donkey, even though God is also unlike this beautiful donkey. Only claims of a wholly univocal sort are to be ruled out, for example, God *is* this donkey.

Nor does our method fall into "a begging of the question," the gratuitous assumption of having established that which one sets out to show while not having in fact shown it. No one has ever succeeded in "proving" the reality of God, for all the splendor of the classical "arguments" for God. Only if *all* theology could be said to "beg the question" of God would we have to apply that condition to the present approach to God. Yet there does remain, of course, a sense in which we *are* "begging the question": No life story of God can ever really—in its essence—be told. However, we do dare to go on and recount the story anyway—in close company with any and all human beings who put forward one or another truth-claim of an imponderable kind (for instance, theoretical astrophysicists). If Jeffrey Burton Russell is right that only the existence of thought can be affirmed with certainty—in the middle of the night I sometimes doubt even that—we may with Russell allow and even encourage ourselves to seek after knowledge that is less than absolute.[10]

Finally, the procedure I am pondering with you does not bring the God-humanity relation down to a human being-puppy dog relation. Instead, it draws the puppy up to a level alongside things wondrous and divine. Since when is a puppy any less a mystery than God? Since when is a puppy any less a miracle than things divine?

Perhaps we may look upon the foregoing heuristic way to God as a comic one, a work of comic vision—not unlike the life we live with the pet we laugh over, but whose absence or death must bring us great grief. In "Peanuts," two small boys sit looking up at the starry night. One of them observes, "Carl Sagan says there are a hundred billion stars in our galaxy, and there are a hundred billion galaxies, and each galaxy contains a hundred billion stars! Sort of puts things in perspective, doesn't it, Charlie Brown?"

But Charlie Brown replies: "I miss my dog."[11]

The modest knowledge to be evoked here is not sentimentality. It is allied to love. That evocation may help us a little to live, to have our being, to laugh, perhaps even to die.

Notes

1. Juan Ramón Jiménez, *Platero y Yo: Elegía Andaluza. 1907–1916* (Buenos Aires: Editorial Losada, S.A., 1942), 33.
2. Consult *Time* cover story, "Can Animals Think?" (22 March 1993), 54–61. The magazine's scientific response is "Yes, and maybe even lie and play politics." In this connection, consult also Dorothy L. Cheney and Robert M. Seyferth, *How Monkeys See the World: Inside the Mind of Another Species* (Chicago: University of Chicago Press, 1990); and Donald R. Griffin, *Animal Minds* (Chicago: University of Chicago Press, 1992). I have no interest in dichotomizing humankind and

animalkind. "In contrast to 'lesser' forms of nature, a new kind of being [the 'higher' animals] confronts reality and us, a creature that gathers impressions all its own and matures into rudimentary self-consciousness and self-identity. Here are creatures who are eligible for deprivation and pain, but capable as well of a certain childlike companionship together with its fateful partner, loneliness" (A. Roy Eckardt, *For Righteousness' Sake: Contemporary Moral Philosophies* [Bloomington: Indiana University Press, 1987], 327). For that matter, I should not wish to dichotomize humankind and the remainder of creation. See, in this connection, Eric W. Gritsch on Martin Luther and being "in tune with creation" in *Martin—God's Court Jester* (Philadelphia: Fortress Press, 1983), 190–94; also Harold H. Oliver, "The Neglect and Recovery of Nature in Twentieth-Century Protestant Thought," *Journal of the American Academy of Religion* 60 (1992): 379–404; and Mark I. Wallace, "The Wild Bird Who Heals: Recovering the Spirit in Nature," *Theology Today* 50 (1993): 13–28.

3. Eckardt, *For Righteousness' Sake*, 328. Further to the animals, consult Andrew Linzey, *Christianity and the Rights of Animals* (New York: Crossroad, 1987); Charles Pinches and Jay B. McDaniel, eds., *Good News For Animals? Christian Approaches to Animal Well-Being* (Maryknoll, N.Y.: Orbis Books, 1993); and William J. Short, "Restoring Eden: Medieval Legends of Saints and Animals," *Continuum* 2 (1992): 43–57.

4. It is, however, wrongheaded to rule out the presence of morality, that is, the reality of good and evil, right and wrong, within the natural world. As I look out my study window I see a small house finch perched next to our garden pool and obviously quite unafraid of two much larger mourning doves out for a stroll very close by. Mourning doves are very good—from the house finch's point of view, not mine (although I do rather agree with the finch). Were a blue jay to arrive, the finch's wings would beat a hasty exit. Blue jays are not very nice: thus testifies the house finch. The finch is, with all winged creatures and many other creatures, a thoroughly moral being, engaging in judgments of good and evil every day, every moment. I speak only empirically. Eugene B. Borowitz puts it just right: "All morality begins with self-preservation."

5. Marcel Gutwirth, *Laughing Matter: An Essay on the Comic* (Ithaca and London: Cornell University Press, 1993), 3.

6. On the other hand, Marcel Gutwirth points out that laughter "is rigorously incompatible with awe" (ibid., 17). Here God would seem to be in pretty good shape— for God hardly has to be awestruck by the Devil or by anyone else.

7. E. M. Schorb, "Destruction," *The American Scholar* (Spring 1993): 234.

8. In the Exodus account, the best that God seems able to come up with is, "I AM WHO I AM" (3:14). What could our Hollywood people ever be expected to do with *that*?

9. G. Tom Milazzo, *The Protest and the Silence: Suffering, Death, and Biblical Theology* (Minneapolis: Fortress Press, 1992), 16.

10. Jeffrey Burton Russell, *The Devil: Perceptions of Evil from Antiquity to Primitive Christianity* (Ithaca and London: Cornell University Press, 1987), 258.

11. *Allentown* [Pa.] *Morning Call* (16 July 1993).

4

Before the Beginning, In the Beginning

God is in His crystal palace.
I mean that it is raining,
Platero. It is raining.
　　　　　　　—Juan Ramón Jiménez

Once upon a time there was a God.
Wrong.
Once upon a time there was God.
Still not quite right.
Once upon a time there was, is, and will be God.

Such is the major presupposition of the present study, an assumption freely admitted to be undemonstrated, indeed undemonstrable, though yet not incoherent with this or that dimension of human experience (such as comedy).[1]

I recall an aphorism from the psychoanalyst Henry A. Murray, a revered teacher of mine: "There are reasons to distrust a truth that forms a sect."[2] I doubt that the "truth" to be put forth in this chapter will run much danger of eventuating in a sect. Yet, who knows? There are very strange sects around. And people do believe some very wild things.

I

The title of part II of this book is "Pages From the Life Journey of God: The Middle One or Two Years." "Pages from" is meant to signify incompleteness. Shamefully, I seem to have mislaid many of the pages of God's history that I ought to be bringing to your attention. Also, I may as well own up that I have not been allowed access to a number of the eligible pages, not yet at any rate.

I have the temerity to say "*the* life journey of God" but only because "*a* life journey" strikes me as a bit timorous. People who write for publication are supposed to have accumulated *some* measure of self-confidence, while yet managing to avoid vainglory. In the latter regard I call attention to the modest remainder of my section title, "The Middle One or Two Years." By contrast, in entitling his entire study *The Early History of God,* Mark S. Smith shows a lot more nerve (chutzpa) than I could ever muster.[3] And Karen Armstrong goes beyond both of us, calling her book simply *A History of God.* "A" sounds cautious enough, but "History" remains wholly unqualified.[4]

On the other hand, perhaps all such wordings simply outdo one another with respect to their absurdity. Were exclusive emphasis to fall upon the eternality of God, upon God's nonhistoricalness—yes, hardly a provable assertion, any more than is God's historicalness—it would be out of the question to link the coming of the Israelites with the early history of God, or even with my much more delimited exercise in the divine history.

I may make reference here to a slight but weighty volume called *God: The Ultimate Autobiography.*[5] In doing so, I hope that the reader will not take me "too seriously" yet at the same time that the point I wish to make will not be remanded to sheer fantasy (cf. our relating of comedy and myth in chapter 2).

God: The Ultimate Autobiography is reputed to be "copyright Jeremy Pascall," but clearly Pascall is an impostor. Did you ever hear of a God with the name Jeremy? Jeremy Pascall simply wants in on the divine action. (Do you mind a little digression here? I was also surprised that the language God resorts to is English; I had always been taught that God spoke Irish. And I still believe that God is very largely Irish, this on two grounds: [a] where but in Eire have literature and politics achieved a mix incendiary enough to satisfy God? and; [b] Recently I heard that whenever Irish people were forced to leave their homeland, they thought of the move not as emigration but as exile [*fogradh*]. Apparently, God does not emigrate either. But sometimes God does go into exile [as declared by the Jewish Kabbalah]. All in all, God's complete family line is Irish/Jewish, though, I am told, with some mix of Muslim-Arab thrown in. However, Anthony Towne, editor of *Excerpts from the Diaries of the Late God,* declares that internal evidence persuades him "that God *thought* in Aramaic."[6] But remember, Towne is dealing with a *late* God.)

To begin to come, at last, to my point; At the very end of God's auto-biography we are supplied, not unfittingly, with a page headed by the words "In the Beginning..." just as, naturally, a similar page has al-ready appeared in the front. The end-page reads:

> In most autobiographies the subject starts at the beginning, but in My case that's tricky. I have no beginning. And for that matter, I have no end. I'm Infinite. [God is a mite careless here; better that God should say "Eternal." Infinity is in the first instance a spatial/transspatial, even mathematical, concept, whereas eternity is a tem-poral/transtemporal concept. However, God may not have all that much use for philo-sophic/theologic niceties.—A.R.E.] So it makes starting the story difficult. Not to mention ending it. In theory this book could continue indefinitely which...Haven't I written this bit before? That's the trouble with being Infinite [*sic*], you never know whether something's already happened or is about to happen.[7]

On the other hand, the closing paragraph of Professor Smith's work contains a hint that his phrase "the early history of God" may have a certain legitimacy (as may, by inference, my own wording, "the middle one or two years")—simply because the usage involved in both cases is not unbiblical:

> Yahweh exercised a variety of roles, even sometimes conflicting ones, to the detri-ment of the cults of other deities. Yahweh sometimes embodied apparently contra-dictory capacities. Yahweh was seen as manifest in nature and beyond nature; Yahweh was sometimes anthropomorphic and yet beyond humanity. Imaged in the human person yet only partially imaginable, Yahweh was a deity sufficiently powerful both to protect and punish Israel. Yahweh was equally a personal deity, whose pain matched Israel's pain. Yahweh consoled Israel, answered Israel, and loved Israel.[8]

Only were we forced to contemplate God as entirely nonhistorical would we be forbidden to assign time frames to the deity. Against the finding that the words "the early history of God"—or, for that matter, "the life journey of God"—are perforce absurd, there arises the hope that the history and life of God may be in some sense influenced by dealings with "the other," the human being (as with, in all probability, other beings). Thus may God even come to change the divine mind in consequence of the entreaty of a mortal servant (e.g., in Gen. 18:22-33). With the coming of humanity, at least two histories—maybe three, if you count Old Scratch[9] (see chapter 6)—are under way in (and beyond?) this world. (I take it there are at least a solid gezillion additional worlds going on somewhere/ elsewhere.) Human beings may even manage to blow up this particular world and end their own part in world history, an eventuality that could be construed in opposite ways: as a little embarrassing, or not in the least embarrassing, to You-Know-Who:

> Why do the nations conspire,
>   and the peoples plot in vain?
> The kings of the earth set
>   themselves,
> and the rulers take counsel
>   together,
> against the Lord and his
>   anointed, saying,
> "Let us burst their bonds asunder,
> and cast their cords from us."
> He who sits in the heavens laughs;
> the Lord has them in derision (Ps. 2:1-4).

(What would happen were the stipulation made, "*She* who sits"? Would the laughter be as derisive?)

It is possible, then, to contend that without humankind, God might not be quite the same God, or, more carefully, might not be acting in exactly the same way. All this suggests a redoubtable question: Could our telling of God's story somehow have an effect upon God, if only a modest one?

II

In *The American Scholar,* journal of Phi Beta Kappa, Aristides has provided an editorial essay called "Such Good Taste." I esteem the writings of Aristides, particularly when, as often, he waxes witty and does so in such good taste. I applauded the entire essay until I came to the assessment of the "new" *New Yorker,* at which place I found I had a bit of a problem. The *New Yorker*'s "inherent good taste" under William Shawn's long and distinguished editorship is praised. But now, alas, the magazine has, according to Aristides, come under an aesthetic/moral cloud. William Shawn would never sanction "four- letter words or other profanities." Nor would he publish stories "that described or talked about fornication, plain or fancy." Today, by contrast, one is turned away by the "childish obliviousness" of *The New Yorker*'s "attempts to outrage."

It is as if "a fine and reliable old friend...has, in his senility, discovered a novelty store and suddenly taken to pulling various obscene objects out of his pockets: rubber vomit, inflatable sex organs, plaster of paris dog droppings."[10]

The justification for my seemingly extraneous allusion to Aristideedeezzes's discomfort with *The New Yorker* is the episode's bearing upon the ethics/aesthetics of "pages from the life journey of God." Aristides would doubtless lament the impending fall of the present book into poor taste via things scatological, shortly to protrude in the present chapter. Incidentally or not so incidentally, Enid Nemy earnestly argues for "tack" over "poor taste"; she finds "poor taste" "too tasteful." Nemy is irresistible in her three levels of tack: light (as in "pity they don't know better"); medium or regular (perhaps a highly visible Phi Beta Kappa key [note my seemingly offhanded reference to *The American Scholar* above]); and low/high (actions that demand such a judgment as "disgusting").[11] Oddly enough, at least for many readers, I want to assign burping (as per below) to low/high tack (certainly when it is public), whereas I retain a strange hate/love relation to "----ing" (guess what?).

I am myself a bit disappointed that *The New Yorker* is not quite the funny, even uproarious magazine it once was. Gone are the hale and halcyon days of E. B. White, James Thurber, and company. On the other hand, these are the 1990s, an entire century away from the 1890s. What was once severe "poor taste" may not be just that today. If it is so that beauty is in the eye of the beholder (to be sure, not only there[12]), so too taste is in the mouth of the consumer. The adage, *de gustibus non est disputandum*—or, for that matter, *de disgustibus non est spitoondum*—continues to exert considerable force. Evangelists for "good taste" are left in the plight that good taste is perforce *their* good taste. And that's the rub.

Contemporary prissiness is reminiscent of the gnostic notion that things bodily and earthy are suspect, even downright defective, while the only really uncontaminated dimension of life remains that of mind and spirit (a traditional, if happily waning, ideology amongst academics). As Harold Bloom writes, the "unwitting Gnostics" of the present "follow the ancient heresy of believing that the Creation and the Fall were one and the same event."[13]

I must, in praise, give voice to Marcel Gutwirth's work once more:

The comic open secret: beneath my underthings there is to be found a body, complete with "secret parts," and it both shits and pisses.... Writing in the final decade of the twentieth century, I enjoy the freedom (at least I take it so) of naming these functions by their more explosive onomatopoeic names, a breach of decorum for the sake of comic expressiveness which I expect my readers to forgive. Not so long ago such an expectation would have been thought worse than fatuous, such a liberty licentious. It is hard therefore to gainsay that part of the comic force of such usage derives from the lifting of inhibitions; that the body excremental, in other words, operates in the literature of scatology that rather operatic maneuver dear to the heart of today's hermeneutes, the return of the repressed.[14]

Were *On the Way to Death* to boast a single aim—and why can it not do that?—that aim would be: Down with repression!

And yet.

There is a slight problem here, in no way respecting the heroic struggle against repression, but only with word usage.

I greatly fear that I am being picky. The last thing I wish to do is cross scatologic swords with my learned colleague Marcel Gutwirth (a distinguished professor of the French language yet). But are the linguistic instances he adumbrates equally or even forcefully onomatopoeic in character? I cannot speak for Professor Gutwirth, or for anyone save myself, and yet I can do no other (in the name of Martin Luther or, even more appropriately, that of Kalsifarr Gebroggian) than testify that my own "p------" and "s-------" either tend to remain almost eerily silent or simply do not sound forth as onomatopoeically as they perhaps ought. And yet, with Marcel Gutwirth's testimony in hand, I am now becoming more and more convinced that, in both instances, my condition must be a terrible aberration, a conspiracy of silence if there ever were such, nothing less than a fatal mutation. We could almost say: a failure of the Word to get itself heard. (Almost needless to add, my "-------" is quite another matter, and is indeed the one bodily act that saves me from the conclusion that my strange quietude is without exception.)

In any case, the theological quality of the stinkweed/tree of heaven that is beginning to bloom here—courtesy of Gutwirth, Eckardt, and how many others—bursts into full smell via the query, What is the relation of God and nature? Is it so, for instance, that human excrement is offensive to God? Is so-called fornication unexceptionally, *inherently* evil? If so, is not a split opened arbitrarily between God and the honesties, imperatives, and exigencies of actual life? (I am shaken to learn, courtesy of *The Random House Dictionary,* that "stinkweed" and "tree of heaven" are one and the same. I trust this is not a portent. Could Heaven stink? I hope to heaven [*sic*] that it was someone other than God who said, "I stink, therefore I am.")

Consider, in contrast to the Manichean heresy, this passage in *Excerpts from the Diaries of the Late God*:

> Blast that Myrtle! She's supposed to be my secretary, not my nursemaid. Every month when a new *Playboy* comes up from down there the dratted woman removes the centerfold before hurling what's left into my IN box. I, to whom all hearts are open, all desires known, and from whom no secrets are hid, am denied, by a meddlesome frump, erotic titillations available to any prep-school freshman. But I fixed her wagon. Plump in the middle of this morning's routine taped dictation I slipped a delicious limerick, a most amusing trifle—picked up from John XXIII—about the Bishop of Birmingham and a boy from Bulgaria.[15]

I might concede that in his prefatory caveats to the *Excerpts,* Anthony Towne accepts that some entries in the diaries "fall outside the bounds of good taste," while others "would, I fear, be deemed heretical in some circles."[16]

But perhaps the most grievous element within a prudery of silence is its unconscious retention and furtherance of certain unruly passions of our psyche—if you will, a sort of analising of discourse. The slogan of the ragged 'sixties, "Let it all hang out," probably reflected and also catered to poor taste—excuse me: tack—yet at least it acted to offset a little the destructiveness of Victorian repression. Be it noted in this regard that, in marvelous whimsy, the one who now sits in William Shawn's editorial chair (once removed) at *The New Yorker* is—a woman!

III

I shall try to work with the foregoing dilemma of good taste versus tack by applying it to the problem of God-language. For to speak or write of God, construed as the One who finally meets us, is to face, not alone the question of the relation, if any, of God and the world, but as well the issue of "right" language—the propriety of language, the morality of language. The issue of acceptable or advisable language is central, of course, within any subject, not just in theology or in the philosophy of religious faith.

The form of God-language I shall utilize in the remainder of this chapter but also elsewhere is underwritten by the unproven, perhaps mad assumption that God is our Friend—however much we are driven by the woes of life to know God also as our Enemy—together with a corollary premise that between good friends, what appears to be sacrilege may not be that at all. Either this phase of the book will smack of indecency in the worst degree (reducing *The New Yorker*'s reputed transgressions to child's play) or the analysis will go, paradoxically, to obviate sacrilege under the aegis of a friendship ecstatic enough to open itself to fantasy and absurdity. As we noted above, the psalmist has God laughing (2:4); once that *line of daring* is crossed, who or what is there to forbid additional bodily functionings to God? When the Zen sage Yun-men (862–949) found that the Buddha is "a wiping-stick of dry dung," was he being blasphemous or was he simply announcing that he had come to find himself at peace with the universe?[17]

In keeping with the basic assumption stated at the beginning of the previous paragraph, God-language may be flavored, licitly, with all-out comedy. It is the case that two principles, the norm of free expression and the standard of decency, very often conflict. Yet each has its place. It is my conviction that among comedy's many blessings is its bringing of a measure of peace to that conflict, without any sacrifice of either of the principles. In this way, comedy can be a minister of goodness, perhaps even an arm of divinity. I have cited Elayne Boosler: Comedy itself arises from our need for justice.

Solely within the above frame of reference, it may not be illicit to joke about God. The dual question is: Are we grown up now? And is God grown up? I believe that authentic personal dignity for humans (also for God?) goes hand in hand with free self-expression and self-respect[18]—two vital implementations of the *imago dei*. Considered overall, religious faith may underwrite values that appear as opposites: self-acceptance vis-à-vis self-humiliation. One obligation of faith is to foster the first of these while working to humble self-sufficiency so that it may come to avoid self-idolatry. (Yet cf. Wylie Sypher: The comic contains an element of blasphemy.[19])

IV

In a more sustained shift from sobriety into the mood of comedy/humor, let us see how the orientation I've been talking up may be brought to bear upon a single episode in the life story of God: the creating of the universe.

I suppose that one of the more incongruous sides—I tend, as already mentioned, to be attracted to the (not uncontroversial) incongruity interpretation of comedy[20]—to any effort to fabricate a complete life story/ life journey of God is the lack of both a birth record and a death notice. Nobody seems to know—I have been conducting exhaustive inquiries in the United States and enquiries in the United Kingdom—when or where, if ever or somewhere, God was born (not to mention the identity of possible parents or kin) or when or where, if ever or somewhere, God may have died (despite all the pronunciamentos of the so-called death-of-God people).[21]

The best we can do is to expatiate upon a particular historical segment, viz., the middle one or two years (or minutes) of God's life. ("Middle" may be a little presumptuous.) In light of the fact that the end of things has evidently not yet been implemented, I shall refrain from any reporting on that kind of business, resisting as I must constantly do certain strong impulses to prognostication. We may recall the world-class watchword, first pronounced by Sledgio of Fflaw in 1119: Shallow eschatology is no match for deep scatology.

Refreshingly enough, the initiating of the universe turns out to be not all that difficult to describe. In *Excerpts From the Diaries of the Late God* (cf. the Early God of Mark S. Smith), we are afforded a beginning clue, small but telling:

> Sitting in the garden this morning, after tea, [22] staring into the deep as I have done more mornings than I could count on the flicks of my eye, [23] suddenly there came to me, as though out of nothing-*ex nihilo?*—a thought so simple and yet so profound I fancied I had experienced an emotion.
>
> *I am that I am.*
>
> Could ultimate truth be reduced to a mere gritty kernel? What troubles me, however, is the utter simplicity of the thought, which has to be accounted either metaphysical or merely redundant. What does it mean? I do not know, but somehow can't escape a feeling of anticipation. Candor compels me to confess it: finally, after all these futile eternities, finally and suddenly, perhaps because I have chosen a new blend of tea, I seem to be on to something really big!
>
> *I am so full of myself I think I could create a world.*[24]

At least two admissions are in order: (1). The *Excerpts* can hardly claim the authority of the primary source *God: The Ultimate Autobiography,* wherein God stipulates that even the Bible is, at best, an unauthorized biography.[25] The *Excerpts* are, in this connection, saddled with the deflating name of an earthling editor, and an Englishman at that. (The truth is I love the English, and I am very happy with God's choice of Anthony Towne as God's own editor. Rather remarkably ungrudging for a God who is so largely Irish.) (2). Jussively, the above citation ends not with an act but with no more than a thought.

Nevertheless, the quoted passage contains a highly significant clue well worth following up: *What God eats and drinks may have decisive import for the very eventuality of creation.*

In final preparation for my disclosure of the exact Method of Creation, I am forced to interrupt the proceedings and turn a bit personal. I have to own up to a certain squeamishness, probably a leftover from my Victorian conscience, my gnostic past, and hence my secret kinship with Aristides. However, I do not go so far as to accuse myself of prudishness. That would be out of the question—on the transparent basis that I am a male. (The same applies, of course, to Aristides.) For according to *The Oxford Dictionary,* the word "prude" may well be traceable to *prudefemme,* a woman of extreme propriety but usually with the meaning of affectation. *Prudhomme,* contrariwise, refers strictly to an upright, honest man, while even more revealingly, *prudhomie* means integrity. Q.E.D. (You will protest: This is nothing more than sexism in action, French style. And you are right. Confidentially, men are, in truth, *les cochons, n'est-ce pas?*)

What I am leading up to is that we are about to be propelled into the whole miasma of the divine flatulence.[26] There, I finally managed to get it out. I have used up all my delaying tactics. But I do wish to God (NB) that somehow we all could have been spared this finding. I've got all I can do even to *think* about so fulsome a phenomenon. You can imagine, therefore, what this must mean for my peace of soul in the matter of that immeasurably more odious, yet I fear ultimately unavoidable, popularization, "----." I can't bear even to reproduce its initial letter, let alone the whole dreadful word, all this despite the common usage the word has gained among all males and even some females (probably not excepting, I weep to conjecture, Miss America and Miss Universe).

It might settle us down a bit and also afford us better perspective if the crosscultural evolution of certain terms is made clear. Expectably, the American *Webster's Dictionary of English Usage* refuses to admit to its listings not only "----," but even "flatulence." Being British, and hence in notably greater rebellion against Victorian Gnosticism, *The*

Oxford Universal Dictionary is more accepting of things blastworthy. It allows places for both "----" and "flatulence," although respecting the former it does confess "not in decent use." Accordingly, "flatulence," first surfacing in 1711, would seem the more appropriate characterization—did it not possess, as we shall see a little later, a fatal empirical flaw. Curiously, the adjective "flatulent" made its appearance much earlier, going all the way back to 1599. The horrible four-letter thing did not come in to the language until 1632.

Our apperceptive mass is at last complete enough to bring us directly to the subject at hand. Put more honestly, we have no choice but to face the truth of creation and its exact mode.

We come back to the clue singled out above—the consequence of the divine diet for the eventuality of creation—and we do so via a reference to *The New York Times*. (For some, the *Times* is The Authority, much more than any mere diary or even autobiography of God Godself.)

The event of creation is epitomized in a recent account, a page one story in the *Times,* boasting the headline, "Scientists Say Satellite's Findings Confirm Big Bang Cosmic Theory."[27] Cosmologists today, so the *Times* reports, assert with overwhelming certainty that recent infrared measurements confirm "the basic Big Bang theory as the best explanation of how the universe began some 15 billion years ago."

The historic science-religion controversy has been dealt a mortal blow. For on the theological side we have long retained an exact counterpart to the Big Bang within the English Bible (even if one that is solidly sexist, though perhaps not unfittingly so: *Vivent les cochons!*): "He makes his wind blow, and the waters flow" (Ps. 47:18).[28] True, Scripture fails to point out—and I had to wangle this piece of intelligence via a special divine confession while You-Know-Who was only half-awake—that on the very evening before creation God was served for dinner a massive assortment of (precreation) legumes, genus *Phaseolus*—quite savory little eospheres yet possessed of portentous, explosive capability.

The rest is history.

This dietary report serves two divergent though equally weighty truths. It describes the mode of the creation of the universe, yet in doing so it manages to keep the science-religion dialogue from falling into total eclipse. For our scientists and religionists are left with plenty of raw materials for mutual discussion—though only before and after, and never during, dinner.

V

It remains for me to offer a pair of midrashim.

1. *Descent into eructation?* There is always some joker around who wants to spoil things: "It was not a ----, it was a burp." (Please telephone my psychiatrist and ask her how I am able so unhesitatingly to write "burp," yet have great trouble with its brother "-----.")

What the joker has done is to treat woodenly and overliterally (cf. our understanding of myth) God's reported reference to having drunk a new blend of tea, and also to assign undue significance to God's observation that God is so full of Godself that God thinks God could create a world. (Whew! The battle against sexism is weighing us down with an awful lot of "Gods.") The joker has absolutized God's simple change of tea blend, while totally ignoring both the entry of "perhaps" in God's diary and the wholly hypothetical "think I could" in God's presumed conclusion.

In stellar contrast, there is nothing at all speculative or less than apodictic in the pristine declaration, God "makes [God's] wind blow."

We do have to concede that "eructation" came in as far back as 1607, and that's a little over a hundred years before "flatulence." However, this does nothing whatever for the shaky hypothesis of eructation. That entire concept is simply disgusting—in Enid Nemy's phenomenology, a case of low/high tack.

2. *Flatulence at bay.* It can at last be asserted that "flatulence" itself incarnates a fateful difficulty. Not that there is any derivational problem; *flatulentus* means "a blowing" (contra Nirvana, a blowing *out*). Fine. The problem is, instead, connotational/experiential.

Simply put, the phenomenon before us—and, even more so, behind us—suggests, empirically treated, roundulence and not flatulence. Just consider the universe as such: Granted, it is not overweight. Yet it is anything but flat. It manifests no less than four dimensions, possibly more. A cause is always proportional to its effect, and vice versa. God finds Godself *"full of myself,"* scarcely a beggarly one- or even two-dimensional description.

I am quite aware of Professor Isless Flaubert's conjecture that one sensible way to account for the popularity of "flatulence" is that the initial human act of this kind must have taken place while the person was seated, and in a particularly closefitting chair at that. A less bizarre, superficially more plausible suggestion is that of Professor Show And Telluride of Lapland, who, in a lengthy though in the end dispirited treatise, traces the triumph of "flatulence" to a conspiracy engineered in the seventeenth century by the Roundheads. This group lived under the illusion, typical of idealists, that only "we" have achieved total descatologization, while "they" only keep on flatulating. (You will perhaps excuse the neologism; it is occasioned by my fanatic hatred of "----" and "-------.") The one piece of positive evidence Telluride is able to introduce is that the Flathead Indians of northwest Montana unexceptionally refer to the act in question as roundulence.

This latter datum seems extraneous.

Or does it?

No, it does not.

Let's hear it for Big Bang Roundulence as well as for various small bang roundulences all 'round the world—these latter the one wholly unambiguous, completely pure, fully scientific *imitatio dei*.[29]

Should you desire, dear reader, to provide us with a wiser and more convincing accounting of the start of the universe—a more lovable myth—1 shall consider trading in my tale for yours. But I would plead, perhaps needless to hope, that you avoid the vulgarity of eructation. Tacky, tacky.

VI

I think I have the reader's attention now. The question is: Can I hold it? By "letting the metaphor of the world as God's body try its chance," Sallie McFague gives evidence of operating on a wavelength not different from ours. For in her very next sentence she allows that "we are experimenting with a bit of nonsense to see if it can make a claim to truth."[30] In chapter 2 I made a small pitch in behalf of nonsense. Nonsense does not have to mean frivolity. And I have just exemplified intensively the *Anschauung* of nonsense via the Divine Roundulence, with its clear linkage of the world to the body of God, a claim that has direct and positive bearing upon the question of evil and the terror of death. (The nonsense here has a lot more going for it than the competing docetic nonsense that the universe is an aspect of pure thought.)

The general theory that shapes up here is called *panentheism,* not to be confused with pantheism. Historically, panentheism (*pan,* all; *en,* in;

theos, God) is congruent with the biblical dialectic of God's transcendence/immanence—together with God's personhood—whereas pantheism tends to sacrifice transcendence to immanence. In deism of the "absentee landlord" variety divine transcendence is irrefrangible. Panentheism falls between this form of deism (also classical theism) and pantheism. It is not that God and "all things" are one, but rather that "all things" somehow live (and also die) within the being or compass of God. The existent world is relatively and proximately, yet not ultimately, independent of the essential deity. Everything created depends upon the Creator; the Creator is not finally dependent upon the created.

The voice of panentheism is heard in the land these days, conspicuously though not only amongst feminist thinkers. Thus, Elizabeth A. Johnson notes that in contrast to classical theism, for which "the world exists always and everywhere 'outside' divine being," as well as to pantheism, for which any "radical distinction between unoriginate mystery and creature is blurred," panentheism offers "a model of free, reciprocal relation: God in the world and the world in God while each remains radically distinct."

> The accent on divine relatedness to the world overcomes the isolation of the patriarchal God of classical theism. At the same time positing relation as the principle of self-distinction thwarts the tendency toward absorption that marks the stereotypical feminine of pantheism.... What [the panentheist] model brings into view is a dialectic in which human beings are created *capax infiniti* and the mystery of God perdures as *capax finiti,* capable of mutual relation with what is not divine. The world then, although not necessary in a hypothetical sense, does make a difference to God. She would not be creator, vivifier, redeemer, liberator, companion, and future without it.[31]

The nonsense I have put forth may, however, offer some moral advantage over a more serious (congruous?) metaphor of the world as God's body-as-such. A friend of mine responded to a summary of my nonsense this way: "Absolutely. We are nothing more than a Cosmic '----.'" (Of course, being free of my hangup, he gave voice to the word itself. I thought immediately of the fact that one of our [*sic*] spiral galaxies contains enough gas to create eight billion stars like the Sun.[32] Our own immediate share in the cosmic "----" is a bit piddling. [Pardon the overstatement.]) If no demand for humility is exigent here, I don't know what such a demand is. At the same time, our condition is not incoherent with a kind of comic thrust that is very hard to find in sacramentalist orientations to the world. Accordingly, our viewpoint may help supply the *imago dei* with a little needed courage: "OK, if that's all we are, here's one for You, Buster!" For the *imago dei* to talk back in this way may itself give voice to God's voice, the poor Dumb One who finds it so difficult to recount the divine story.

None of this insolence—however good a feeling it gives us (God can surely use some advice)—need do anything to make us feel less sorry for God than we would otherwise. I insert a case in point. In human cancers the body appears to be devouring itself. During the very same eon as ours, God's body appears, alas, to be in a closely related plight. According to most recent scientific information, and in particular a report by Douglas N. C. Lin of the University of California, Santa Cruz to the American Astronomical Society, the gravitational force of "dark matter" in the halo of our galaxy "is causing the Milky Way to consume, bit by bit, the stars and gases of its nearest galactic neighbor, the Large Magallanic Cloud 160,000 light-years away." Within a mere twenty billion years, our own Milky Way will have finished this particular meal. In addition, cannibalistic "dark matter" is, according to Michael Turner, the dominating matter in the universe as a whole.[33]

In a word, cancer is as much cosmic as it is earthly/animal—or, as a worst-case scenario, the latter forms of cancer simply mirror self-destruction at the cosmic level, galactic cannibalism.

All you and I needed was a God with a malignancy right there in the solar plexus! I told you we were losers. (Or did I? Well, maybe not using that word.) Is this not a beginning hint that God too is something of a klutz? (Poor God.) There is, however, some consolation, if it can be called such. "The new estimate of [galactic] mass falls short of the proportion of dark matter that astronomers believe is necessary to halt the expansion of the universe."[34] Big Bang Roundulence seems a bit hard to offset. Again, but at the microcosmic level, we have recent word that "radioactive antibodies can hunt down spreading blood cancer" in the human body, destroying all signs of the disease.[35] So it may well be at once unjust and unrealistic to throw up our hands and moan that God is goofing off. She does seem to be staying on the job, probably doing the best She can.

To conclude: From a panentheist perspective, the radical suffering we know in this world does not elude the potential providence of God. If in death we do not fall "outside" God's body, it may be that we are not condemned to meaninglessness after all, since we remain somewhere within God's jurisdiction and care. Can that not serve as a comforting joke for us? Nevertheless: If there are such realities as divine care and even redemption for suffering creatures, these processes operate in ways quite hidden to human beings. Furthermore, such praxis does nothing at all to remove or forgive the terror of death. Minimally speaking, God stands in severe need of a much better operational method than that of death.

Are you interested in proposing, or are you able to propose, an alternative? Please do not hold back. Please do not be anal.

Notes

1. Cf. the old but, for me, not dated work of Douglas Clyde Macintosh, *Theology as an Empirical Science* (New York: Macmillan, 1919); see, upon a particular theological/experiential issue, the more recent monograph by Richard R. Niebuhr, *Resurrection and Historical Reason: A Study of Theological Method* (New York: Charles Scribner's Sons, 1957); and consult the current study by Gordon D. Kaufman, *In Face of Mystery: A Constructive Theology* (Cambridge: Harvard University Press, 1993).
2. Henry A. Murray, obituary of Sigmund Freud in the *American Journal of Psychology* (1940), as cited in Paul Roazen's review of *Love's Story Told: A Life of Henry A. Murray* by Forrest A. Robinson, *The American Scholar* (Spring 1993): 311.
3. Mark S. Smith, *The Early History of God: Yahweh and the Other Deities in Ancient Israel* (San Francisco: Harper & Row, 1990).
4. Karen Armstrong, *A History of God* (New York: Alfred A. Knopf, 1993). However, Armstrong's work is in the first instance a history of *human ideas* concerning God.
5. *God: The Ultimate Autobiography* (London-Sydney-Auckland: Pan Books, 1989).
6. *Excerpts from the Diaries of the Late God* (hereinafter *Excerpts*), ed. Anthony Towne (New York: Harper & Row, 1968), 2.
7. *God,* 136.
8. Smith, *Early History,* 166. The many biblical citations marshaled by Smith in this passage are here omitted.
9. I much prefer "Old Scratch" to "Old Harry." The second designation is offensive to my family and me. I happen to have a cousin named Harry, and he is a very fine person. Few people are named Scratch. But some are named Sam Hill, as was the case with an old colleague of mine. So I suggest we eliminate the latter moniker as well, an American euphemism for the Devil. One favorite of mine is the name Bubonic Plagiarist, which has the advantage of standing among the Devil's own self-descriptions (*Satan; The Hiss and Tell Memoirs* [London-Sydney-Auckland: Pan Books, 1989], 13n).
10. Aristides, "Such Good Taste," *The American Scholar* (Spring 1993): 176. Parts of the remainder of the present chapter first appeared under the title "Blastoff," in *Satire* 1, 3 (Winter 1994): 46–51.
11. Enid Nemy, "Richter, Move Over for the Tacky Scale," *The New York Times* (20 May 1993).

12. In *Excerpts*, of which more anon, we are advised, "Beauty is *not* in the eye of the beholder. Beautification is" (72).
13. Harold Bloom, "New Heyday of Gnostic Heresies," *The New York Times* (26 April 1992). See also Bloom's controversial work *The American Religion: The Emergence of the Post-Christian Nation* (New York: Simon & Schuster, 1992).
14. Marcel Gutwirth, *Laughing Matter; An Essay on the Comic* (Ithaca-London: Cornell University Press, 1993), 136.
15. *Excerpts*, 22.
16. Ibid., 5.
17. Consult James B. Nelson's useful study, *Body Theology* (Louisville: Westminster/ John Knox Press, 1992).
18. Consult Diana T. Meyers, *Self, Society, and Personal Choice* (New York: Columbia University Press, 1989); also Paul Tillich, *The Courage To Be* (New Haven: Yale University Press, 1952). See in addition Nicholas A. Kuiper and Rod A. Martin, "Humor and self-concept," *Humor* 6-3 (1993): 251–70.
19. Wylie Sypher, cited in George Aichele, Jr., *Theology as Comedy: Critical and Theoretical Implications* (Lanham, Md.: University Press of America, 1980), 34.
20. See John Morreall, ed., *The Philosophy of Laughter and Humor* (Albany: State University of New York Press, 1987). The enjoyment of incongruity "is both necessary and sufficient for humor; no other kind of enjoyment is either necessary or sufficient for humor" (216). See, more extensively, Morreall, *Taking Laughter Seriously* (Albany: State University of New York Press, 1983), chap. 5. For a more recent analysis, consult Giovannantonio Forabosco, "Cognitive aspects of the humor process; the concept of incongruity," *Humor* 5 (1992): 45–68.
21. On the reputed "death of God," consult *Excerpts*.
22. Here is sterling evidence that God is not in fact English. In the morning the English have "morning coffee"; tea comes before breakfast and then again in the afternoon.
23. Is this to intimate that God can boast only one eye? If so, perhaps it is to be denominated the Good Eye—in order to establish a contrast with the Devil's Evil Eye. At the least we now have testimony that God is anything but blind. However, the *Excerpts* assure us that God actually has two eyes, "ovaltine set off against white tending toward a reddish yellow" (24).
24. *Excerpts*, 12 (second set of italics mine).
25. *God*, 10.
26. I regret to have to disclose that *The American Scholar*, over which Aristides presides, has itself allowed the word "flatulence" to invade its pages—and in the very same number as the critique of *The New Yorker* I allude to above: See advertisement by Harvard University Press, Spring 1993, 299. Perhaps a forecast is in order: As Harvard University goes, so will eventually go *The American Scholar*.
27. *The New York Times* (8 January 1993). For two authoritative sources here, useful to the lay person, consult Robert M. Wild, *Space, Time, and Gravity: The Theory of the Big Bang and Black Holes*, 2nd ed. (Chicago: University of Chicago Press, 1992) and Stephen Hawking, *Black Holes and Baby Universes* (New York: Bantam Books, 1993). Even within scientific circles, the phrase "Big Bang" is held to be inappropriate for such a momentous phenomenon as the origin of the universe. The phrase originated as a slur on the part of Fred Hoyle, advocate of the "steady state" theory. In 1993 the astronomer magazine *Ski & Telescope* sponsored a competition for an alternative name. Winners were to be announced in January 1994 (*The New York Times* [11 June 1993]). Since there is no way for this book to

appear until after January 1994, I here apprise you of my entry: The Great Delivery. If I don't win, the judges are stupid. A commentary on the contest in "Sunday," (*The New York Times Magazine* [31 October 1993], 32) criticized the proposed change from "Big Bang" as violating the "heart of the scientific enterprise, which is "a lack of proper respect, for anything but the facts of the matter." What the *Times* does not seem to have learned—or taught its writers—is that many scientists regard themselves and their work as dealing with much more than simple or pure "fact." (P.S. to the above: In March 1994 *Sky and Telescope* announced that nobody had won the competition.)

28. We must not allow ourselves to be distracted into exploring the fantastic parallelism, as suggested in the psalm, between two divine tracts, the intestinal and the urinary: wind-and-water. But the two together certainly do inspire divine poesy.

29. Consult Richard M. O'Neill, Roger P. Greenberg, and Seymour Fisher, "Humor and Anality," *Humor* 5 (1992): 283-91. That study reports upon an experience involving forty married women. But my own orientation as a male toward anal humor just may typify the investigators' (tentative) findings respecting anal fixation, or linkage to obstinacy, orderliness, and parsimony. However, I think that I am, in fact, much more captive to orderliness than I am obstinate or parsimonious. I might add that a number of years ago a doctoral proposal was made to the Department of Psychology at Lehigh University to study types of human flatulence (pitch, force, frequency, occasion, purpose, etc.). The authorities rejected the proposal, I suppose on grounds of poor taste or perhaps of elusiveness. Query: Why is it that I have never been able to stop laughing over this episode? I have no idea. It certainly was anything but a laughing matter to the unhappy candidate.

30. Sallie McFague, *Models of God* (Philadelphia: Fortress Press, 1987), 69. See also McFague, "Imaging a Theology of Nature: The World as God's Body," in *Liberating Life: Contemporary Approaches to Ecological Theology,* ed. Charles Birch, William Eakin, and Jay B. McDaniel (Maryknoll, N.Y.: Orbis Books, 1990), 201-27. If "world as God's body" is a metaphor, is "God"/God also a metaphor? The fact that I here show uncertainty whether to use inverted commas with "God"/God may hint at a hoped-for answer in the negative. It is a truism that all human words show a metaphorical face, due to the inexorable gap between linguistic expression and what it is that language is seeking to identify or reckon with. It would appear, however, that most users of the word God (*Gott, Dieu, Dios,* et al.) are not thinking/acting in an exclusively metaphorical way, but are proceeding rather more like someone who says, "Tomorrow the noted designer Ezio Tomashoovsky is coming to Wanamakers." The reference is to a particular individuation that somehow exists and does things. Needless to say, when believers sing, "A Mighty Fortress Is Our God," they are treating "Mighty Fortress" strictly as a metaphor (a myth?), since they are hardly identifying God with an edifice made of stone and concrete.

31. Elizabeth A. Johnson, *She Who Is* (New York: Crossroad, 1993), 230-32. See also McFague, *Models of God,* 69-78; and Grace Jantzen, *God's World, God's Body* (Philadelphia: Westminster Press, 1984). Consult Walter Wink, *Naming the Powers* (Philadelphia: Fortress Press, 1984), 124, n19.

32. John Noble Wilford, "Hubble Shows Results of Collision by 2 Galaxies," *The New York Times* (26 May 1993).

33. John Noble Wilford, "Weighing Milky Way, Astronomers Find Halo of Dark Matter," *The New York Times* (8 June 1993).

34. Ibid. In the same account Douglas N. C. Lin provides the additionally humbling (and epoch-making) news that we humans "are not even made of the most common material there is in the universe." Lin assigns as great importance to this discovery as to the discoveries of Copernicus and Herschel.

35. "Radioactive Antibodies Found to Destroy a Cancer," *The New York Times* (12 August 1993).

5

Hither and Yon:
Twenty-One Divine Adventures

I can't be everywhere, can I?
All right, I can but it's very
tiring when you get to My age.
Which you won't.
                                              —God[1]

We have been apprised of the sending of the universes upon their
way: the countdown and the blastoff.

Because of God's problems with "before" and "after," as alluded to
in chapter 4, it is not easy to arrange in correct order the following (highly
fragmentary) selection of God's worldly adventures subsequent to the
creation. The sequence to come is subject to some alteration. In one or
two places I am responsible for interfering with what might be a more
chronological tale. (Some of you will wonder whether the choice of
adventures reflects a particular theological bias. Perhaps I can just say:
We tried to work things out together; there was political give-and-take.
God is a good politician, and I try to be one. In the latter connection,
most of the subheads are mine.)

HUMANKIND, ANIMALKIND

"I was only making someone who could do odd jobs around the garden."
"Look at it this way, I'd already put most of My energies into creating the really
important animals, the ones I'd intended would rule My new planet."[2]

HOW GOD ENABLES NATURE TO FUNCTION

How is it possible that blades of grass flourish so well and sprout so evenly?

An old Jewish tale has each and every blade attended by an angel who whispers "grow!"

Midrash: The modern world was to come along and claim that a given blade of grass is in essence no different from any other blade. "Thereby was lost the marvel of grass. The postmodern opportunity will sanctify each and every blade of grass" through a reminder that "each has been assigned its special angel."[3]

THE EXODUS

On the appointed night I sent the final horror into Egypt—The Plague of Encyclopaedia Salesmen.

And it came to pass that they knocked on the door of every Egyptian house but they did not approach the doors daubed by the Israelites. And faced with this terror Pharaoh called Moses and said to him, "Okay, I know when I'm beaten. You and your people and herds can go, as long as you take those salesmen with you."

And Moses said, "Rejoice in the name of the Lord, for this is the time of our exodus."

And Pharaoh said, "What does 'exodus' mean?" And Moses replied, "Look it up in your encyclopaedia."[4]

NO TIME FOR SINGING

When the Holy One, blessed be He, decided to drown the Egyptians at the Red Sea, the guardian Angel of Egypt stood before the Lord and pleaded: "Lord of the universe, Thou hast created the world with mercy as its measure." The guardian Angels of all the other nations sought mercy for the Egyptians. Whereupon the Angel Michael signaled to Gabriel, who flew to Egypt and removed a brick from the wall of a building. Within the brick was the immured body of a Jewish child. And the Angel Gabriel went and stood before the Lord and held the brick forward, and said: "Behold: this is what the Egyptians would do to Your children." Whereupon the Holy One, blessed be He, dealt with the Egyptians in strict justice and determined that they deserved their fate. But when the Egyptians were drowning in the Red Sea, the ministering Angels began to sing songs of joy. Whereupon the Lord rebuked them, saying: "My creatures are drowning in the Sea; how dare you sing before Me?"[5]

COMMANDMENTS, COUNTERCOMMANDMENTS

Once upon a time God resolved to show the people of God how to live. Particularly directed to the children of Israel, the Decalogue is reputed to be applicable in certain ways to humankind as a whole:

Then God spoke all these words: I am the Lord your God, who brought you out of the land of Egypt, out of the house of slavery; you shall have no other gods before me.

You shall not make for yourself an idol, whether in the form of anything that is in the heaven above, or that is on the earth beneath, or that is in the water under the earth. You shall not bow down to them or worship them; for I the Lord your God am a jealous God, punishing children for the iniquity of parents, to the third and the fourth generations of those who reject me, but showing steadfast love to the thousandth generation of those who love me and keep my commandments.

You shall not make wrongful use of the name of the Lord your God, for the Lord will not acquit anyone who misuses his name.

Remember the sabbath day, and keep it holy. Six days you shall labor and do all your work. But the seventh day is a sabbath to the Lord your God; you shall not do any work—you, your son or your daughter, your male or female slave, your livestock, or the alien resident in your towns. For in six days the Lord made heaven and earth, the sea, and all that is in them, but rested the seventh day; therefore the Lord blessed the sabbath day and consecrated it.

Honor your father and your mother, so that your days may be long in the land that the Lord your God is giving you.

You shall not murder.

You shall not commit adultery.

You shall not steal.

You shall not bear false witness against your neighbor.

You shall not covet your neighbor's house; you shall not covet your neighbor's wife, or male or female slave, or ox, or donkey, or anything that belongs to your neighbor (Exod. 20:1-17).[6]

The divine life journey is hardly represented fairly without some provision for things that have happened *to* God upon the way. We exemplify this latter area in the present chapter. (The question of the *convergence* of divine acts and human acts comes to a climax—only for Christians, of course—in Jesus of Nazareth and the Incarnation.)

Once upon a later time, an unidentified "American prisoner" devised "the other half of the Covenant: a layman's decalogue to God."[7]

> Thou shalt love man as much as man loves thee.
> Thou shalt honor thy promise to Noah.
> Thou shalt protect all children from every natural harm.
> Thou shalt ease childbirth's travail.
> Thou shalt match man's pace toward peace.
> Thou shalt not cause the birth of crippled children.
> Thou shalt not steal children from their parents.
> Thou shalt not cause the poor, the innocent or the faithful to suffer famine.
> Thou shalt not harden any man's heart.
> Thou shalt not test one man more than any other man.

Scripture is replete with punishments for human disobedience of God's Decalogue and other commands. We shall have occasion in succeeding pages to reckon with the question of the punishment to be directed to God for the many violations of our unknown soldier's apodictic decalogue, plus additional divine wrongdoings. For the present, I might point out that the unknown soldier goes fairly easy on God. For instance, he ignores such specters as cancer and such evils as his own coming death. Accordingly, we may add a minimum of two items to the list (readers may want to supply others):

Thou shalt destroy cancer, AIDS, and like horrors. And do be quick about it.
Thou shalt obliterate the terror of death.

In singling out these two supplements to the list, and with especial reference to the
latter one, we may have particularly in mind Job's observation:

> It is all one; therefore I say,
> he destroys both the blameless
> and the wicked.
> When disaster brings sudden
> death,
> he mocks at the calamity of
> the innocent (Job 9:22-23).

However, this torah from Job—constituent, after all, to the biblical canon—suggests
at least two further additions, not to the soldier's decalogue, but to God's Decalogue:

To supplement my ninth commandment: You shall also be unreservedly honest
with me.
To emend my second commandment: You are to love me all right, but it's
okay if you hate me sometimes.[8]

Pierre Wolff would be quite sympathetic to such additions as these. He declares:

Father, when I suffer I cannot help crying out, questioning, asking a thousand
whys, like a child without self-control or understanding. I am sure you listen to
me as a father patiently and lovingly listens to his child. You do much more,
because you are *the Father* "from whom every fatherhood...takes its name"
(Eph. 3:14). So I am giving you all of this: my revolt, my resentment, my hatred,
even though they are directed at you.

Once during a retreat someone...said to me, "It was difficult for me to give up
to the Lord my anger and hatred because I wanted to *choose* the gift I would give
the Lord. I was so happy and proud to offer my patience, my care for people, my
love. I wanted to choose beautiful shoes in which to meet him. He showed me the
kind of shoes that were for me: they were ugly and worn but they fitted my feet
perfectly, so that I could walk and run toward him with ease. So I took *my* shoes,
I gave *my* gifts; I gave over to him *my* anger and *my* hatred."[9]

(How distressing that our brother Pierre should, of all people, maleize God! But the
Gospel of Luke helps erase this trespass [shared by Jesus himself? No, Jesus' century
was not the twentieth]: "Father [*sic*], forgive them; for they do not know what they are
doing" [Luke 23:34].)
In case you wish to know my own reaction to all this, I can easily provide it: The
score to this point is 12-12, and it's now the sixth inning. I have a feeling we will be
going into extra innings (as per the contents page which, however, is trying to play

God to future history when in fact the chapters to come haven't as yet been worked out. How can the contents page know something the author does not know? That takes more than psychokinesis. It takes a special kind of guile.)

Am I wandering off from the life journey of God?

No. God's problem is precisely that of being stuck with human tiresomeness, human nastiness, human foibles, human freedom—and inhuman writers. But: We did not originate that state of affairs. God did. For we never asked to be born.

DEFLATION HITS BOTTOM

Before the Torah was given to the Children of Israel, God offered it to all the other nations of the earth so that they could not complain later, "If only You had offered it to us first, we would certainly have accepted it!"

The first nation to whom God offered the Torah asked, "What is in this Torah?"

God said, "You shall not murder."

They quickly rejected it, for they said, "We live by the sword."

The next nation asked, "What is in it?"

And God replied, "You shall not commit adultery."

And they also refused it, for they said, "We are all the children of unchastity. How could we accept this Torah?"

The third nation asked, "What is in it?"

And God said, "You shall not steal."

They laughed and shook their heads, for they said, "We make our living by robbing each other blind. This Torah of Yours is not for us!"

The next nation asked, "What is in it?"

And God answered, "You shall not lie."

They rejected it rudely, for they said, "We cannot give up the law of our fathers, for they have taught us to shun the truth and profit by deceit."

And so it went with all seventy nations of the earth. Each one rejected the Torah, since to accept it would mean changing their ways completely, which they were unwilling to do.

Then God came to Israel, and said, "Will you accept My Torah?"

What is in it?" they asked.

"Six hundred and thirteen commandments."

And they said, "All that God has spoken we will obey and we will hear."

God was pleased with their words and gave Israel the Torah for an inheritance throughout their generations.[10]

What if the people of Israel hadn't been elected the Chosen People?

Some other people would have got it in the neck.[11]

GOD'S ENCOUNTER WITH RACHEL

In the work Lamentations Rabbah, Rabbi Samuel bar Nahmani tells of God's decision to send the Israelites into exile in Babylon. Successively, Abraham, Isaac, Jacob, and Moses plead with God, all to no avail. Finally Rachel leaps to the fray. Her intervention concludes: "You are the King, living and enduring and merciful. How come then you are jealous of idolatry, which is nothing, and so have sent my children into exile, allowed them to be killed by the sword, permitted the enemy to do whatever they wanted to them?"

In response, "the mercy of the Holy One, blessed be He, welled up, and He said, 'For Rachel, I am going to bring the Israelites back to their land.'" For Scripture tells, "Thus said the Lord: A cry is heard in Ramah, wailing, bitter weeping, Rachel weeping for her children. She refuses to be comforted for her children, who are gone. Thus said the Lord, Restrain your voice from weeping, your eyes from shedding tears; for there is a reward for your labor, declares the Lord, they shall return from the enemy's land, and there is hope for your future, declares the Lord: your children shall return to their country" (Jer. 31:15-17).[12]

A WORD FROM THE LAND OF SYRIA

"Ephraim the Syrian constructed a dramatic dialogue in which Death, Gehenna, Sheol, and Satan all lament the death of Jesus, which they had hoped to use against God and humanity but which he cleverly turned against them."[13]

SEQUEL TO A DEATH

The Romans murdered Jesus of Nazareth, Jesus the Jew.[14] Subsequently, we are told:

After the sabbath, as the first day of the week was dawning, Mary Magdalene and the other Mary went to see the tomb. And suddenly there was a great earthquake; for an angel of the Lord, descending from heaven, came and rolled back the stone and sat on it.... For fear of him, the guards shook and became like dead men. But the angel said to the women, "Do not be afraid; I know that you are looking for Jesus who was crucified. He is not here; for he has been raised, as he said. Come, see the place where he lay. Then go quickly and tell his disciples. He has been raised from the dead, and indeed he is going ahead of you to Galilee; there you will see him."...So they left the tomb quickly with fear and great joy, and ran to tell his disciples, "He has been raised from the dead." (Matt. 28:1-2, 4-9).[15]

GOING DOWN

"Jesus Christ...was crucified, dead, and buried; he descended into hell."[16]

What was God doing in hell? Or at least God's *Stellvertreter*? Pierre Wolff offers one response: "In sorrow no place exists that the Lord cannot now reach."[17]

GOING UP

"...The third day he rose again from the dead; he ascended into heaven, and sitteth on the right hand of God the Father Almighty...."[18]

I have two problems here.

1. "Sitteth"? In this relatively early time, how could God already be propagating Elizabethan English?

2. Does God really favor the divine right hand? I was brought up to believe that God is left-handed, along with all good first basemen.

ONCE WHEN GOD WAS FORCED TO SMILE

Rabbi Eliezer ben Hyrcanus used every argument in the world to support his opinion that a certain oven was ritually clean, but the other rabbis opposed him.

He said, "If the *halakhah* [way to go] is with me, let this carob tree be uprooted from the earth!"

And the carob tree rose into the air and flew five hundred feet before it crashed to the ground. But the rabbis said, "You cannot prove anything with a carob tree."

Then he said, "If I'm right, let this stream of water flow backwards!"

And instantly the stream reversed its course and flowed the other way.

But the rabbis said, "A stream can't prove anything." Then Eliezer ben Hyrcanus shouted, "If the law is with me, let the walls of this study house prove it!" And the walls immediately began to teeter, but Rabbi Yehoshua reproached them and said, "Is it any of your business, walls, if scholars disagree about the Law?"

And out of respect for Rabbi Yehoshua, the walls stopped falling. But out of respect for Rabbi Eliezer, they did not right themselves either. Thus they remain tilted at an angle to this day.

Then Eliezer raised his voice and called out, "If the *halakhah* is with me, let heaven itself prove it!"

And a heavenly voice rang out, "Why are you opposing Rabbi Eliezer? Don't you know that the Law is always as he says?"

Rabbi Yehoshua now jumped to his feet and cried, "The Torah is not in heaven!" What did he mean by that?

Rabbi Jeremiah explained, "The Torah was given to Israel on Mount Sinai. Therefore, we need not listen to heavenly voices, for the Torah itself teaches us that the majority rules in matters of Law."

Later, when Rabbi Nathan met the prophet Elijah, he asked him, "What was God's reaction to Rabbi Yehoshua's outburst?"

Elijah replied, "God smiled and said, 'My children have gotten the better of Me! My children have bested Me!'"[19]

TO REDEEM OR NOT TO REDEEM

The Berditchever[20] called over a tailor and asked him to relate his argument with God on the day before. The tailor said: "I declared to God: You wish me to repent of my sins, but I have committed only minor offenses: I may have kept leftover cloth, or I may have eaten in a non-Jewish home where I worked, without washing my hands.

"But You, O Lord, have committed grievous sins: You have taken away babies from their mothers, and mothers from their babies. Let us be quits: You forgive me, and I will forgive You."

Said the Berditchever: "Why did you let God off so easily? You might have forced Him to redeem all of Israel."[21]

ON DUTY

One Rosh Hashanah the Berdichever Rebbe searched for someone to blow the *shofar*. He asked each one who came forward, "What are your mystic thoughts when you blow the *shofar*?"

None of the answers he heard pleased him.

Finally one man came to him who confessed that he was unlearned and had no mystic thoughts.

"Then what do you think about when you blow the *shofar*?" the Berdichever asked him.

"I think of my four unmarried daughters who need husbands," the man replied. "I say to God, 'I am doing my duty to You by blowing the *shofar*. Now You do Yours for me.'"

And the Berdichever chose him to blow the *shofar* that year.[22]

A THOUGHT THAT NAGS GOD
UPON RETIRING FOR THE NIGHT

"Sometimes I think if I hadn't revealed anything to them they would have worked it all out much more sensibly."[23]

THE PRAYER LIFE OF GOD

Said R. Yohanan in the name of R. Yosé, "How do we know that the Holy One, blessed be he, says prayers?"

Since it is said, "Even them will I bring to my holy mountain and make them joyful in my house of prayer" (Isa. 56:7).

"Their house of prayer" is not stated, but rather, "my house of prayer."

"On the basis of that usage we see that the Holy One, blessed be he, says prayers."

"What prayers does he say?"

Said R. Zutra bar Tobiah, "May it be my will that my mercy overcome my anger, and that my mercy prevail over my attributes, so that I may treat my children in accord with the trait of mercy and in their regard go beyond the strict measure of the law."[24]

HOW GOD CHOSE THE SITE OF THE TEMPLE

On Mount Moriah in Jerusalem there once lived two brothers. One had a wife and children; the other was unmarried. They all lived together in one house in perfect harmony. Each day the two brothers would rise early and together work their fields.

When it was harvest time, they reaped their grain and brought the sheaves to the threshing floor. There they divided the sheaves into two equal piles and went home.

That night the brother who had no family said to himself, "I am alone, but my brother has a wife and children to feed. Why should my portion be equal to his?"

So he rose from his bed and went to the threshing floor. He took some sheaves from his own pile and added them to his brother's.

That same night, the other brother said to his wife, "It is not right that my brother has the same number of sheaves as I. For I have a greater share of happiness since I have a wife and children, but he is all alone. So the brother and his wife went secretly to the threshing floor and put some of their own sheaves on the single brother's pile.

The next morning the two brothers rose early and went to thresh their sheaves. Both were astonished to find the piles still equal. That night they both went again to the threshing floor and met each other there. When they realized why they were both there, they embraced and kissed each other.

That is why God chose their field as the site of the Holy Temple, for it was there that two brothers showed their great love for each other.[25]

Midrash: In and through its anticipation of my (unmarried) brother Robbie's great kindness and love toward me, I am enabled to call this event the most decisive of the adventures of God here retold. For in this way I remember together the Temple of God and my brother. And I understand why the Temple had to be located in just this field.

THE BIRTH OF THE MESSIAH

"On the day the Temple was destroyed, the Messiah was born."[26]

ONCE UPON A SABBATH

Two Hasidim came to the city of Kallo on the eve of the Sabbath and joined the Rabbi of Kallo for the coming celebration. Unexpectedly, a young man and a young woman knocked at the door and were invited to join the company.

After the [Sabbath] meal the Rabbi of Kallo rose and said: "This couple has come here to be wed this day. And I have agreed to wed them." Now these words were a deep shock to the visiting Hasidim, for weddings are forbidden on the Sabbath....

At that moment the Rabbi of Kallo turned to the two Hasidim and addressed them. He said: "Of course, the consent of everyone present is necessary if the wedding is to be performed. Please tell us if we may have your consent?" And there was almost a pleading tone in his voice.

Now it is one thing to witness such a desecration and quite another to perform one. But the two Hasidim did not dare turn down the *tzaddik* [righteous one] to his face. Instead they each dropped their eyes and...a great fear was in their hearts.

At last, when they raised their eyes, they saw that the couple was gone. The Rabbi of Kallo was slumped in his chair. For a long time there was silence. At last the rabbi said: "Do you know who they were?" Each of the visiting Hasidim shook his head to say no. And the rabbi said: "He was the Messiah. She was the Sabbath Queen. For so many years of exile they have sought each other, and now they were together at last, and they wanted to wed. And, as everyone knows, on the day of their wedding our exile will come to an end. But that is possible only if everyone gives his full assent. Unfortunately, you did not, and the wedding could not take place."[27]

Midrash: Professor Schwartz refers to the parallel between the feminine figure of the Shekinah as Bride of God and C. G. Jung's archetype of the anima, "the symbolic feminine aspect of every man." One of the roles of the Shekinah is to be mother of Israel.[28]

RESPECTING THE DAY OF JUDGMENT

"Said Rav: 'On Judgment Day a man will have to give account for every good thing which his eye saw and he did not enjoy.'"[29]

THE STORY IS ALL

When the great Rabbi Israel Baal Shem-Tov saw misfortune threatening the Jews it was his custom to go into a certain part of the forest to meditate. There he would light a fire, say a special prayer, and the miracle would be accomplished and the misfortune averted.

Later, when his disciple, the celebrated Magid of Mezritch, had occasion, for the same reason, to intercede with heaven, he would go to the same place in the forest and say: "Master of the Universe, listen! I do not know how to light the fire, but I am still able to say the prayer." And again the miracle would be accomplished.

Still later, Rabbi Moshe-Leib of Sasov, in order to save his people once more, would go into the forest and say: "I do not know how to light the fire, I do not know the prayer, but I know the place and this must be sufficient." It was sufficient and the miracle was accomplished.

Then it fell to Rabbi Israel of Riszhyn to overcome misfortune. Sitting in his armchair, his head in his hands, he spoke to God: "I am unable to light the fire and I do not know the prayer; I cannot even find the place in the forest. All I can do is to tell the story, and this must be sufficient."

And it was sufficient.[30]

Notes

1. *God: The Ultimate Autobiography* (London-Sydney-Auckland: Pan Books, 1989), 9.
2. Ibid., 38, 40. The *Excerpts from the Diaries of the Late God* (hereinafter *Excerpts*) contain this note: "Anyhow, Dr. Aquinas, should you wish to inform yourself *accurately* on the post-Fall history of the Garden of Eden, I respectfully refer you to: S. T. Livermore's (The Rev.) HISTORY OF BLOCK ISLAND, Rhode Island. Originally printed 1877; reproduced and enhanced by The Block Island Tercentenary Anniversary, 1961. Printed by facsimile, with addenda, by The Murray Printing Company, Forge Village Massachusetts. Library of Congress No. 61-17173. Price $2.50" (New York: Harper & Row, 1968, 43).
3. A. Roy Eckardt, *Reclaiming the Jesus of History* (Minneapolis: Fortress Press, 1992), 44. To the prophet Muhammad, every falling raindrop is accompanied by its own angel. Cf. Walter Wink: "Every blade of grass, every rock crystal, acorn, and ovum has its '*angelos*' (messenger) from God to instruct it in its growth,

however we name it (DNA, the 'laws' of crystalline formation, etc.)" (*Naming the Powers* [Philadelphia: Fortress Press, 1984], 121). The *Excerpts* maintain that much pseudoscholarly rot has been written on the subject of whether angels exist. The Late God's answer is: "If angels did not exist I would have to invent them, which comes, perhaps, to the same thing. What more can I say?" (70).

4. *God*, 99.
5. Talmud, *Sanhedrin* 39.
6. In Ellen Frankel, *The Classic Tales: 4,000 Years of Jewish Lore* (Northvale, N.J. and London: Jason Aronson, 1993) we read: "As a parting gift, God gave Adam and Eve the Torah as a tree of life, since they were now leaving behind the Tree of Eternal Life. 'Only hold fast to it,' God urged, 'and you will one day find yourselves back in Paradise'" ("The Fall of Adam and Eve," 31; for sources of the tale, see ibid., 611). It is further told that at Mount Sinai "the first word God spoke was, '*Anokhi*': 'I am.' This was not a Hebrew but an Egyptian word. Why did God address the people in Egyptian? To welcome them back after their stay in a foreign land, for when people travel far from home, it is natural for them to become accustomed to a foreign tongue and to forget their own" (*Classic Tales*, 127-28; sources, 615).
7. The wording here is as found, together with the ensuing ten countercommandments, in Pierre Wolff, *May I Hate God?* (New York: Paulist Press, 1979), 4. Were I ever to be coerced into commending *one* book only to others who are "on the way to death," *May I Hate God?* would be the book. That is saying a lot for myself, because I would much rather commend one of my own books. However, I could never tell which one of mine to choose. So I have decided to stay with Pierre Wolff.
8. See ibid., 32 ff.
9. Ibid., 47, 51.
10. Frankel, *Classic Tales*, 122-23; sources, 615.
11. Dahn Ben-Amotz, as cited in A. Roy Eckardt, "Is There a Christian Laughter?" *Encounter* 53 (1992): 111.
12. As recounted in Jacob Neusner, *Telling Tales* (Louisville: Westminster/John Knox Press, 1993), 110-15. "A man should always take care not to distress his wife, for women's tears are close to the heart of God" (*Bava Matsia* 59a, as cited in Hyam Maccoby, compiler and translator, *The Day God laughed: Sayings, Fables and Entertainments of the Jewish Sages* [New York: St. Martin's Press, 1978], 77).
13. Jeffrey Burton Russell, *Satan* (Ithaca and London: Cornell University Press, 1987), 176.
14. From all we can tell, this was because, historically put, Jesus was acting as a revolutionary in behalf of the coming Reign of God, or, from the Roman standpoint, as a seditionist (cf. Eckardt, *Reclaiming the Jesus of History*, 58-61, 71-72, 75, 77-79, 87-88; in general, chap. 5).
15. This is only part of the accounting in the Gospel of Matthew. The other three Gospels provide alternate renderings of the event of the Resurrection.
16. From the Apostles' Creed.
17. Wolff, *May I Hate God?*, 44.
18. From the Apostles' Creed.
19. Frankel, *Classic Tales*, 305-06; sources, 621. I have already utilized this story in *How To Tell God From the Devil*. So if you are so good as to read more than just the one book, you are rewarded by hearing this inimitable tale twice.

20. Rabbi Levi Yitzhak of Berditchev (1740–1809 C.E.). Transliterated spellings of the name vary, which explains the slightly different spelling in the ensuing adventure.

21. As cited in Anson Laytner, *Arguing With God: A Jewish Tradition* (Northvale, N.J. and London: Jason Aronson, 1990), 184, from I. Ashkenazy, ed., *Otzroth Idisher Humor* (1929).

22. Frankel, *Classic Tales,* 509; sources, 627.

23. *Excerpts,* 54.

24. Babylonian Talmud *Berakot* 7A, XLIX, as cited in Neusner, *Telling Tales,* 134–35. In *The Classic Tales* God in one place raises a question about prayer, at least lengthy prayer, responding as follows to a long entreaty from Moses at the Sea of Reeds: "Moses! The sea blocks the way, the enemy is almost upon them, and you stand there praying! My children are in trouble. Sometimes long prayer is good, but at other times it's best to be brief" (114; sources, 614).

25. Frankel, *Classic Tales,* 241–42; sources, 619.

26. Ibid., 338; sources, 623.

27. A nineteenth-century tale from Hungary, in Howard Schwartz, compiler and ed., *Gabriel's Palace: Jewish Mystical Tales* (New York: Oxford University Press, 1993), 251–52; source, 348.

28. Schwartz, *Gabriel's Palace,* Introduction, 25, 19.

29. Palestinian Talmud, *Kiddushin,* end, as cited in Maccoby, *Day God Laughed,* 24.

30. This is the epigraph to Elie Wiesel, *The Gates of the Forest,* trans. Frances Frenaye (New York: Avon Books, 1967); on sources see Frankel, *Classic Tales,* 629. See also Wiesel, *Souls on Fire: Portraits and Legends of Hasidic Masters* (New York: Vintage Books, 1973); and *Somewhere a Master: Further Hasidic Portraits and Legends,* trans. Marion Wiesel (New York: Summit Books, 1982).

6

Fall of God—Angel of Death—
Triplets of History

Is the life journey of God a comedy, or is it something else?

Let us suppose that this life journey is trying as hard as it can to be a certain kind of comedy, viz., to do whatever is possible to counter Suffering with Joy.

I

The trouble is that the horror of evil and the terror of death do not abate. It was by hanging himself that my only brother met death in 1940 when he was just twenty-five. For me, it is an event of today, of this morning. *God, do you have something to say to this? Have you done anything with it? Do you intend to do something about it, or are you content to sit around on your fat buttocks [see below] making universes and arranging marriages?* For Francis of Assisi, melancholy—the affliction of my brother—comes straight from the Devil.[1] The block that has to make us stumble here, yet also St. Francis, is that the Devil is the Shadow of God. So, in ultimate honesty and accuracy, melancholy is from God.

There now, I have indeed "let it all hang out." Yet I plead pastoral support from Father Pierre Wolff as represented in the previous chapter, counsel from his little book *May I Hate God?*

The correct pronunciation above is bYOO-tocks, with a nod to the old musical *South Pacific.*

Yet how could I possibly fling in so crazy an item at so dreadful a place? I do it with the most critical of warrants: Rapid-fire transmogrifications within human sentiment at once establish and reflect the depth of the incongruity involved. Tears are all at once laughter; laughter is all at once tears. Comedy quickly acts to fight back at anguish; anguish quickly acts to fight back at comedy—here is the overall contention of the book, really, as I believe is the case with comedy as such. The *élan vital* moves in to counter and demolish all hard-and-fast categories. The stage explodes. There has to be some way that we are kept from losing our minds.

One role of the variation upon comedy that is directed against the self is comedy's struggle against the ideological degeneration into self-exaltation and self-pity of such artless passions as grief. Yet when I read George Aichele, Jr.'s finding that an "element common to most or all comic theories is the understanding of the basic emotional thrust of comedy as aggression or hostility,"[2] I doubt that I could ever of my own power exempt myself from this charge, with special reference to my relation to God. Human comedy directed against God may very well spring from the aggression that arises from human claims to superiority. However, we cannot rule out the possible justification of such comedy as grounded upon the conviction that God just may fail to live up to God's (*not* humankind's) own standards of what is righteous and good. (Of course, we must concede the eventuality that God's reputed moral standards may themselves turn out to be no more than human fabrications—although such an eventuality may well remain forever beyond knowledge or verification.[3])

Arthur Koestler is on to a great deal when he makes comedy that form of the act of creation wherein "bisociation" occurs: There is simultaneous action on a double plane, entailing two "habitually incompatible frames of reference." Koestler continues: "Before *homo ridens*, the laughing animal, could emerge...a level of evolution had to be reached where thought could detach itself from feeling and...confront its glandular humours with a sense of humour. Only at this stage of 'cortical emancipation' could man perceive his own emotions as redundant, and make the smiling admission 'I have been fooled.'"[4] However, I should think we ought to go on from bisociation to multisociation, for example, God → buttocks → bYOO-tocks, and so on and so forth, ending up, perhaps, in unabashed zaniness (or in nonsense, which is for me the apogee of the comic). Insofar as "bYOO-tocks" and their parallels are enabled to put suffering to shame, if only for a fleeting instant, a galactic victory is won over the blackness of life—excuse me, I mean its whiteness.[5]

II

The main intent of this particular essay among the others is to give voice to the dialectic "Divine Fall"/"Angel of Death," in the hope, not of claiming final reckonings with either category and their relation, but rather of orienting us toward a third consideration. We have, in outline form:

A. The "pact" with Satan.
B. The paradoxical concept "Angel of Death."
C. The import of A and B for Divinity, Humanity, Deviltry at the point of consanguinity.

At the price of oversimplifying, perhaps even of misrepresenting, God's life journey, I have omitted or at least postponed until now any exposition of the Divine Fall. I have done so because of: (a) the particularly weighty significance of this phenomenon for evil and death; and (b) its direct linkage with the three chapters (7–9) that follow this one. Furthermore, we do not know when the words of the epigraph to this chapter (Job 1:12) may have first been uttered. One influential estimate comes out on the near side of 700,000,005 gezillion minutes after the creation of humanity—approximately one eighth of a divine year. We could spend a full scholarly day working out the connection between that space/time and the historical composition of the Book of Job, the latter perhaps during the period of the Babylonian Exile in the sixth century B.C.E.

In addressing in chapter 4 the question of the authorship of *God: The Ultimate Autobiography,* we observed that Jeremy is not a very convincing candidate for the divine name. There is additional, telling evidence that the words "copyright Jeremy Pascall" are bogus. For the fact is that another book, published under the very same cover with *God* (but printed upside down; I kid you not), carries the self same copyright, and this one is titled *Satan: The Hiss and Tell Memoirs.*[6]

It is to be questioned, some will say, whether God and Satan (the Adversary) come down to one and the same individuation.

But is it to be questioned?

Our old uneasiness may return when we once more recall the Jungian psychoanalytic asseveration of the Devil as Shadow of God.[7] The uneasiness is compounded when we think again of Jeffrey Burton Russell's authoritative judgment (already identified as an overall watchword of the present book but also, and perhaps more significantly, one that is buttressed by nothing other than Latin phrasing): "The study of the Devil indicates that historically, he is a manifestation of the divine, a part of the deity. *Sine diabolo nullus Deus.* Yet, morally, his work is completely and utterly to be rejected."

More exactly, I repeat from chapter 1, now not in passing but instead with stress—what a marvelous word that can transfigure into one flesh the realities of "emphasis" and "anguish"—upon the historical identification of Devil and Death. The Epistle to the Hebrews attributes to the Devil "the power of death" (2:14), thus raising up a special ensign for us: the Devil as commanding Death. Can we not then extrapolate: The Shadow of God is Death, whereas God driving beyond the Shadow, God in God's no-longer-repressed integrity, is Life? The war against Death is seen to be part of the war against the Devil,[8] and God participates in this war, both as culprit for evil and as soldier against evil.

The beginning of the Book of Job provides explicit guidance respecting the first of our three themes, the Fall of God. According to the poem's prose prologue,

> one day the heavenly beings came to present themselves before the Lord, and Satan [the Accuser] also came among them.... The Lord said to Satan, "Have you considered my servant Job? There is no one like him on the earth, a blameless and upright man who fears God and turns away from evil." Then Satan answered the Lord, "Does Job fear God for nothing? Have you not put a fence around him and his house and all that he has, on every side? You have blessed the work of his hands, and his possessions have increased in the land. But stretch out your hand now, and touch all that he has, and he will curse you to your face." The Lord said to Satan, "Very well, all that he has is in your power; only do not stretch out your hand against him!" So Satan went out from the presence of the Lord (Job 1:6, 8-12).[9]

The two parts of God's spoken consent are not easy to reconcile. Possibly Job's *life/fate* is being distinguished from his *possessions* (a distinction actually stated in 2:6). But then we are brought up short by the verse from Hebrews and its subsumption of the power of death under the power of the Devil. However, our concern here is not with the specifics and knotty problems of the dialogue with Satan, or with the subsequent misfortunes of Job in the poem as a whole, or, for that matter, with the wider lessons of the tale in its entirety. We are concerned with only one thing, an incredible thing: the readiness upon the part of God to have some kind of intercourse with the Devil. God does not act to dissociate God from evil. Thus are we left with no choice but to speak of the Divine Fall. (This state of affairs is not inconsistent with other biblical passages. There is Isaiah's frightening attribution of evil to God, cited in chapter 2, "I make weal and create woe," while the Deuteronomist's subsequent switch in sequence does very little to lessen the terror: "I kill and I make alive/I wound and I heal" [Deut. 32:39].)

Did God think through what God was getting into? Was God taking into account the gravity of a pact with the Evil One? How consequential, even deadly, would such a pact be?[10] Perhaps we may at least agree, even those of us who shy away from ontic identifications, that there is good reason for finding God and the Devil to be—how shall we put this?—in cahoots.

With this collaboration or cooperation as a given, I offer one query and four not-unrelated midrashim, all of these pertinent to—surprise!— a blessed eventuality of there being something for us to appreciate in God's "pact" with Satan.

1. Was not God talking to Godself (broadly understood)?

2. It might be going a bit far to sing *O felix culpa diaboli!* much less *O felix culpa dei!* Nevertheless, the affinity of God and Devil appears (speaking psychomorally) to be of aid respecting a certain essential need of ours. I refer back to the moral/existential desirability of escaping from, on the one hand, dualism and its hopelessness and, on the other hand, monism and its unrealism. Needless to add, such an escape does nothing to free us from the terror of evil and death.

3. Beyond the happy finding that sin and evil precede human transgression (as per chapter 1), we are here authorized to stick out our tongues at an evil Devil without quite having to stick them out at God. This is very helpful. Indeed, I have a funny idea that God had this sort of opportunity in mind for us when setting up that little deal with Satan. Does this not offer legitimate support to our breaking out in song, *O felix culpa diaboli*? And in this regard, the Divine Fall may be said to go *up* as much as it goes *down*.

4. An added midrash accords with an essential thrust of this book. The many protestations in behalf of Job's blamelessness that are put

forward in the course of the Book of Job rest upon an impossible foundation. They are tied both to his inner spirit of integrity and to his outer good behavior. But in fact there has never been any such human sinlessness as this; humankind is as much fallen as is God and the Devil. Insofar as he was committed to making Job blameless, the writer of the tale ought to have concentrated upon Job's having had no say in his birth. For this is the only fully authentic blamelessness, the only innocence that forever stays unsullied, as it does with each of us. (Come to think of it, not even *the Devil* asked to be born!)

5. Further to the matter of human sinfulness, it is of relevance to mention that the Devil dedicates his own autobiography *Satan* to Pride, Anger, Envy, Lust, Gluttony, Greed, and Sloth. To the list of sins that are traditionally held to be "deadly"—Satan dubs them "delightful"—Joyce Carol Oates has argued for an eighth: Despair, calling it, indeed, the one "unforgivable sin." Of like mind, Alfred Gilbey identifies despair as "the worst of all sins because it means you have given up the struggle."[11]

III

Comedy, God, and Devil comprise a highly redoubtable triad, perhaps more than we can handle without falling into narrative and/or analytic death by misadventure. Yet had we been able to get away with just those three elements, they would have actually spelled relief. (This is not an ad for Rolaids.) For the truth is that our existential condition is more complicated than even this triad conveys, for all its complicatedness.

For one thing, we are steadily "on our way to death," in that not only do we have to die, but, worse confounded, we are impelled to *ponder* death as at once portent and reality. What an expenditure of valuable, fleeting time! For another thing, by rejecting the opposing choices of religious monism and religious dualism, we have found ourselves unable to elude Professor Russell's stern historical reminder that the Devil manifests nothing other than the divine. (Is this more than we can endure?) In my phrasing, there is no way "to tell God from the Devil" until we have first conceded their consanguinity. But this finding has also caught us up in the reality of "fallen angel,"[12] entailing, on the one side, an apodictic admission of theological (diabological) evil and yet, on the other side, a preventative of the immorality of loading all culpability for moral evil upon the shoulders of humankind.

Thus is our original triad of Comedy/God/Devil expanded by the intrusion of two further categories, Death and Angels.

This is getting to be a little ridiculous. How are we ever to handle any such quintilectic as this?

All right. Politically, I propose a compromise, in the interests of a little easing of the complexity. I don't know about your brain, but mine is hurting. It is not impossible to think of a working alliance, even a merger, of the two additional variables in question, via convenient assistance from an ironic twinning furnished by the Western religious tradition: *Angel of Death.* Thus may the quintilectic be reduced at least to a quadrilectic. All this gives sustenance to what might be labeled eschatological sick humor: the Angel of Death as expository *consolation*—this, quite free of any incentive supplied by either cancer or AIDS.

Here we can now stand then: Comedy/God/Devil/Angel of Death. Just how does the Angel of Death operate? Not having as yet met that personage face-to-face, I remain a little unsure. Pending such a meeting, I throw out several amplifications and reflections, moving from angel as such (*malakh,* lit. messenger) to fallen angel to Angel of Death.

1. If things divine and things diabolic are alike eligible for the category of myth as a dimension to be taken seriously, how could we exclude things angelic from that category?

2. Angels as such are fun. How could broadly comic endeavor overlook them? Or get along without them?

3. Although angels of Scripture are not wholly identified with God, the angel remains "the messenger of God and speaks in His name, and is often called by the name of Him who sent him. The speech and action are the work of the angel, but the thought or will is God's." This last is seen in such instances as Balaam's donkey (Num. 22:22-35), food for Elijah (I Kings 19:5-8), and the destruction of Sennacherib's army (II Kings 19:35-36; Isa. 37:36-37). (For Rabbi Akiba, angels are outranked by sages.[13] I wonder whether sages are enabled to outrank the demons too.)

4. Geddes MacGregor has given us a study entitled *Angels: Ministers of Grace.* His hypothesis respecting the reality of angels at once accords with traditional religious belief and is "scientifically plausible, however undemonstrable." He suggests that angels may be "more advanced forms of intelligent life" that "could have developed along another evolutionary line to a higher form than ours and be more rational, more benevo-

lent, and so capable of helping humans in the way that angels in traditional religious lore are said to do." MacGregor continues:

> The superego, like all such psychic constructs, is no more than a psychic receptacle
> or receiving set in the use of which I must learn to acquire powers of discrimina-
> tion, as one may find out how to discern, amid the bulk of televised trash, some
> programs of value.... We ask, then, what is the magnet that attracts the human
> psyche "upward" and that is so feebly and sometimes so inefficiently reflected in
> the working of that aspect of it Freud chose to call the Superego? Theists will
> readily answer that of course it is God, which is a neat answer indeed; but we may
> well find more immediately useful the concept of various dimensions of existence
> through which we are passing on our long evolutionary journey that slowly leads
> those of us who are willing to listen to the "angel voices" more and more into
> enhanced awareness of a higher dimension that is already impinging upon us.[14]

With MacGregor's speculation as a working model, it is possible for
us to move from the ratio-and-proportion of chapter 3 ("we are to the
animals as God is to us") to a more complex relation, "we are to the
animals as the angels are to us as God is to the angels."[15]

5. Angels are supposed to be, normally, obedient to God.[16] By definition, a fallen angel betrays the will of God, or strives to do so. (This
presupposes, awesomely, an element of free will within angels.)

Geddes MacGregor's phrase for Satan is "the realm of angels gone
wrong."[17] "The Fourth Lateran Council (1215) declared it is a matter of
faith to be accepted by all Christians that Satan and the other devils are
by nature spirits created by God and therefore originally good, and that
they 'fell into sin of their own free will,' so being 'eternally damned.'"[18]
Yet I venture to repeat: Did the Devil ever ask to be born? Furthermore,
if the Devil is at once blameworthy and unblameworthy, does he (sic)
not join humankind as a thoroughly comic (incongruous) figure?[19] (Additional query: If it is in some measure licit to "fool" with God, is it not
then licit to "fool" with the Devil, Shadow of God?)

MacGregor ends his chapter on Satan with a correlative question:
Once we take angels seriously, do we not have to take with equal seriousness "their demonic counterparts: the 'angels gone wrong'?"[20]

6. The line from angel to fallen angel to the fully outrageous combination Angel of Death (malakh ha-mavet) is a relentless and unbroken
one: When a good angel falls, it falls into evil, and when death descends,
a final evil is manifest.

So here is an oxymoron to beat most oxymorons I've ever seen: In
one moment we fabricate a divine messenger, and we come up with

goodness (*Angel* of Death); in the very next moment we ponder death, and we are dismayed (Angel of *Death*). And would it not be better just to die, or even to get ourselves killed in some stupid accident? Why does there have to be an *Angel of Death*?

Our conflictive and ambivalent existence is thrown into vivid relief in and through the struggle of Moses against death, as represented in the biblical and rabbinic traditions. Germane to our interests is the fact that in the death of this patriarch/prophet questions are raised concerning the justice (or goodness) of death as such. I select a few items from the confrontation of Moses and God.

"To annul the decree of death, Moses draws a magic circle around himself and hurls his prayers to the Heavens. God orders the Gates of Heaven shut but Moses' prayers batter against the gate and set all the angels atremble. To no avail." Having been told in no uncertain terms that he must die without ever passing over the River Jordan into the land of promise, Moses accuses God of making a fraud of God's own Torah, insisting that God incurs guilt by violating Deuteronomy 24:15. Among God's responses is an assurance that Moses will live and be rewarded in the World to Come (*olam ha-ba*). "But Moses clings to life. Defiantly, he takes up writing a Torah scroll and the Angel of Death fears to approach him to take his soul.[21] When ordered to return a second time, the Angel of Death receives a beating from Moses' staff. Finally, God resolves to act and calms Moses' fears directly. *God Himself, not the Angel of Death nor human beings, will attend Moses' burial.* With sweet words God calls forth the soul, and *weeping*, gives Moses the kiss of death" (emphasis mine).

Who, then, is God, in an angelic frame of reference?

God is that Angel who sheds tears in the midst of suffering, and in this way comes clear of the Shadow.

Anson Laytner comments: "Moses may have lost the argument [A.R.E.: Do you know somebody who has *won* it?] but he was comforted by learning and personally experiencing what every human being longs to know—that death is not the end, that God does care, and that He has provided a future beyond the grave in the World to Come."[22]

Each of us, on the way to death, is left with life-and-death questions. Is death just death, lying perhaps within a dimension like unto fallen angel, the dimension of evil and sin? Or is death to be somehow redeemed by God's *Angel* of Death, promising instead the dimension of the divine mercy? Does the Angel of Death range itself, is it to be ranged, within the camp of the Devil (radical evil, radical suffering), or does it appertain to the providence of God (radical good, radical blessing)? It is the terror of death that makes inescapable the angelological question: Is there only hopelessness, or is there hope? Which is to be the victor, meaninglessness or meaning?

<h1 style="text-align:center">IV</h1>

In their convergent aspects, sections II and III of this chapter point toward a third phenomenon: The history of this world gives birth to a synchronism of synchronisms, a strange brood indeed: Divinity/Humanity/Deviltry.

If God hides Godself, if the Shadow hides behind the Shadow, and if even human beings act to hide themselves within themselves, there is nevertheless a certain objective mutuality of experience, a certain common estate. If the world is God's body, God never remains entirely hidden. This is more than can be said for the Devil who, with gangsters everywhere, is always hiding out. Samuel Terrien proposes that instead of speaking of the hiddenness of God, we do better to speak of a presence that is self-concealing.[23] This is a not improper description respecting humankind as well, even perhaps respecting the Devil.

Divinity, Humankind, Deviltry—the triplets of history, of the generations (*toldot*)—carry within their varying morphologies of freedom the single and singular shared mark of accountability (*Verantwortlichkeit*): three moral deciders, three fallen realities, three comic characters, three representations of life and death. One of the players seems uniquely subject and directed to death. Yet in and through such tales as those of Moses and of Jesus an incommensurate possibility comes to birth: Could the Devil (Death, the Shadow) also be marked for extinction? Could the devilish one of the triplets of history be headed toward death in order that, or at least with the result that, another of the triplets might live?

It is a most salient fact that at least two of the characters (Humankind, Deviltry) bring an element of innocence to their fallenness (they never asked to be born), as at the same time they remain fallen and responsible amidst that very innocence (they consort with evil). The Eternal One boasts a certain innocence as well ("Poor God," chapter 3);

however, this innocence is not exactly unsullied: there is a Divine Fall. Indeed, the Devil's evident thrownness into existence itself points, by contrast, to the Divine Fall as Final Fall. For the blameworthiness of God persists as the only ultimate blameworthiness—quite unsoftened and quite unredeemed by any plea of birth-apart-from-volition.

Thus does a specter persist: Crimes have been committed, and they will have to be paid for. The life journey of God moves into the future. That future is fraught with risk, including nothing less than condemnation.

Notes

1. Julien Green, *God's Fool: The Life and Times of Francis of Assisi,* trans. Peter Heinegg (San Francisco: Harper & Row, 1985), 141.
2. George Aichele, Jr., *Theology as Comedy: Critical and Theoretical Implications* (Lanham, Md.: University Press of America, 1980), 37.
3. Consult in this latter connection Karen Armstrong, *A History of God* (New York: Alfred A. Knopf, 1993).
4. Arthur Koestler, *The Act of Creation* (New York: Dell Publishing Co., 1964), 35–36, 63; in general, chaps. 1–4. The other condition of *homo ridens,* says Koestler, is security of existence. See also Aichele, *Theology as Comedy,* 32–33, and Marcel Gutwirth, "Laughter Sparked: A Binary-Stuctural Approach," in *Laughing Matter: An Essay on the Comic* (Ithaca and London: Cornell University Press, 1993). Cf. the old chestnut Koestler links to Schopenhauer, "A convict was playing cards with his jailers. On discovering that he cheated they kicked him out of jail." Along the same line, "honor among thieves" demands condemnation—from the standpoint of thievery. Again: If a thief locks his door upon leaving home, is he not a traitor to his own calling?
5. "Do we really *need* white chocolate? I mean, we blacks don't have very much. Can't we at least have *chocolate*? (Arsenio Hall).
6. *Satan: The Hiss and Tell Memoirs* (London-Sydney-Auckland: Pan Books, 1989).
7. The format of the twin work *God* and *Satan* may comprise, consciously or unconsciously, a bow to Jung. Each part is the flip side of the other.
8. Cf. Eph. 2:1-2: "You were dead through the trespasses and sins in which you once lived, following the course of this world, following the ruler of the power of the air [Satan]" (see also 6:11-12).
9. The *Excerpts From the Diaries of the Late God* offer this alternative account: *"I am bored with it all.*... I am condemned to look out interminably in all directions into an impenetrable void. Small wonder that wretched, horntailed ingrate walked out on me" (ed. Anthony Towne [New York: Harper & Row, 1968], 11). More seriously (?), in the comic visions of such Christian expositors as George Aichele, Jr. and Ralph C. Wood the question arises of whether Christian thinking has been zeroing in so long and so hard upon the alleged universality of the world's (all humankind's) sin—no question of whether the obsession is a magnificent and necessary one— that it is prevented from discerning (a) the darker sin of God, and (b) the historic sin of Christian replacementism (vis-à-vis Judaism and perhaps other faiths). If so, would this suggest that the end product of Christianity is not comedy but tragedy?

10. The commentator for *The New Oxford Annotated Bible* appears to be as unschooled as I in theological diplomacy: "Satan's proposal puts God in a no-win situation. If God refuses, it looks as though he fears there may be a basis to Satan's claim; if God accepts, he comes out of it looking heartless" (New York: Oxford University Press, 1991, commentary on Job 1:11-12).

11. Joyce Carol Oates, "The One Unforgivable Sin," *The New York Times Book Review* (25 July 1993): 1, 25 (last of a series in the *Times* on the deadly sins); Sue Fox, "Alfred Gilbey," *The Times Magazine* (London) (29 January 1994): 54.

12. The "fall" of the Devil (the personification of evil) is not to be confused with the "war in heaven" of Rev. 12:7-9, although there is a relationship. The *Harper's Bible Commentary* provides a helpful paragraph upon the latter happening: "The myth of the heavenly battle in which Michael defeats and expels Satan and his angels (vv. 7-9, a variant version is reflected in Rev. 9:1; cf. *1 Enoch* 90:21) is always a *primordial* rather than an eschatological event in Jewish thought (*2 Enoch* 29:4-5; *Adam and Eve* 12-16; cf. Isa. 14:12-15). Yet Satan's eschatological fall to earth is closely paralleled in the only vision of Jesus preserved in Gospel tradition: 'And he said to them [seventy disciples], "I saw Satan fall like lightning from heaven"' (Luke 10:18 RSV). The fact that Michael is the one who defeats Satan, not the Messiah as in Christian tradition, underscores the Jewish character of Rev. 12:7-9. John's elaborate identification of the dragon in v.9 further suggests his modification of a Jewish source" (San Francisco: Harper & Row [1988], 1313).

13. The Hertz *Chumash*, as cited in Philip Ginsbury, "Angels in Jewish Lore," *Common Ground* (London) 4 (1978): 15; Ginsbury, 15-16. For all its monist (monotheist) stress upon the sovereignty of Allah, the religion of Islam makes large room for angels.

14. Geddes MacGregor, *Angels: Ministers of Grace* (New York: Paragon House, 1988), xix, xxi, 127-128; see also 130-31. Consult in addition ibid., chap. 18, "Why Angels?" Further to the angels, see Walter Wink, *Unmasking the Powers* (Philadelphia: Fortress Press, 1986), especially 69-71, 119, 156-71.

15. Walter Wink writes: "Apparently humans are necessary as intermediaries to the angels: angels' angels!" (*Naming the Powers* [Philadelphia: Fortress Press, 1984], 96). I can see no reason to rule out such reciprocity.

16. Not every angel is all that nice. It is said: "While in the womb, the child learns the entire Torah, and knows it. But when the child enters the air of the world, an angel comes and strikes it on the mouth and thus causes it to forget all the Torah it has learnt" (*Nidah* 30b, as cited in Hyam Maccoby, compiler and translator, *The Day God Laughed: Sayings, Fables and Entertainments of the Jewish Sages* [New York: St. Martin's Press, 1978], 200). This particular angel, it may be proposed, has also hobnobbed with Plato, and again with William Wordsworth. Its name is Squelch.

17. MacGregor, chap. 5, "Satan: The Realm of Angels Gone Wrong," *Angels*.

18. Ibid., 45.

19. On the Devil as comic, consult Jeffrey Burton Russell, *Lucifer: The Devil in the Middle Ages* (Ithaca and London: Cornell University Press, 1986), 233-44, 259-64.

20. Ibid., 52.

21. A Jewish tradition has it that the "Angel of Death may not take a soul when it is engaged in study" ("The Death of David," in Ellen Frankel, *The Classic Tales: 4,000 Years of Jewish Lore* [Northvale, N.J. and London: Jason Aronson, 1993], 213; sources indicated on 618).

22. Anson Laytner, *Arguing With God: A Jewish Tradition* (Northvale, N.J. and London: Jason Aronson, 1990), 63, 65–66; for the biblical and rabbinic sources see notes in ibid., 264–65.
23. Samuel Terrien, *The Elusive Presence* (New York: Harper & Row, 1983), 251.

7

Crime—Trial—Sentence—(Secret)

Reb Dovid Din was sought out in Jerusalem by a man who was suffering a crisis of belief. Whatever Reb Dovid said to him, he disputed. Reb Dovid quickly recognized that it was the man's intention to provoke him, so he restrained himself and refused to be drawn into an argument. He listened and listened to the man, who ranted and raved for hours. At last he said to him: "Why are you so angry with God?"

This question stunned the man, as he had said nothing at all about God. He grew very quiet and looked at Dovid Din and said: "All my life I have been so afraid to express my anger to God that I have always directed my anger at people who are connected with God. But until this moment I did not understand this."

Then Reb Dovid stood up and told the man to follow him. He led him to the Western Wall, away from the place where people pray, to the site of the ruins of the Temple. When they reached that place, Reb Dovid told him that it was time to express all the anger he felt toward God. Then, for more than an hour, the man struck...the Kotel [wall] with his hands and screamed his heart out. After that he began to cry and could not stop crying, and little by little his cries became sobs that turned into prayers.

And that is how Reb Dovid Din taught him how to pray.[1]

I wonder whether when setting out upon the divine life journey, God could have counted upon or even anticipated the singular goings-on we have described down to this point. For God's sake, I rather wish that God could have been spared the downside of the part of the story we have sketched, though not the upside. I should not wish the downside on my best Enemy.

I

It is the terror of death, more than any other evil, that poses the question: Is God the Enemy? Of course, many other evils beset us within the human world: ethnic idolatries, nationalist destructiveness economic exploitation and oppression, misogyny, racism—the list goes on. We could blame only human beings (ourselves) for these corporate evils, and not God. But would not that be too easy, too simple? Geddes MacGregor points out that war, for example, "though human greed and other vices play a part in it, does not seem to be wholly explicable in human terms. War is indeed more like a virus attacking humanity."[2] The same is the case with many other systemic evils of human life. They are ridden with the demonic, fed by the diabolical. And at the ultimate level of reckoning, the God who stands *out there* beyond all the proximate freedom/destructiveness of the Devil and all the proximate freedom/ destructiveness of humankind also stands *in here* as immanent Culprit.

H. Richard Niebuhr describes the state of affairs out of which a most lamentable condition arises. The identity "of faith may be stated in a somewhat Cartesian fashion: I believe (i.e., trust-distrust, swear allegiance and betray) therefore I know that I am, but also I trust you [another human person] and therefore I am certain that you are, and I trust and distrust the Ultimate Environment, the Absolute Source of my being, therefore I acknowledge that He is. There are three realities of which I am certain, self, companions and the Transcendent."[3]

When it is directed to the third of these parties, the status of belief (trust-distrust) may be construed as originative of, and consonant with, Alfred North Whitehead's persuasion that the developing life of authentic religion entails a "transition from God the void to God the enemy, and from God the enemy to God the companion."[4] In accord with Whitehead, Niebuhr alludes to the Christian's "great reconciliation with the divine enemy."[5] Prefatory to my nonsense upon the creation of the universes, I myself intimated a God who is so good a Friend as to overlook what appears to be sacrilege on the part of humans (chapter 4). For the Christian, as for many other faithful people, the divine Enemy is indeed seen to be faithful Friend. Yet an awful fact continues to burden us. What could be more sad than to be taught by life and death, although much more so by death, to insist upon an unavoidable dialectic?: The Enemy who is Friend is also the One who persists as Enemy (the Shadow remains). For if the Friend is in truth *the* Universal One, it is this very Friend who keeps on giving *some kind* of consent to disease and rape, to pestilence and typhoon, to anxiety and hunger, to meaninglessness and despair, to destructiveness and death. God the Friend abides as Void, even as Enemy.

II

The indictment is followed by a trial—what else could meet the demands of justice, the demands of God Godself, the very justice of God (Gen. 18:25)? The trial that is held is not unlike, in fact it may be looked upon as a recapitulation of, a functional-archetypal trial that took place on 25 February 1649 in Shamgorod.[6] The scene is an inn of "a lost village, buried in dust and darkness." The sole survivors of a recent pogrom are the innkeeper and his daughter, "alone and abandoned." Even the gravediggers were massacred. "Hate has won; death has triumphed."

Berish the innkeeper will serve as prosecutor, but who is to serve as defense attorney? Does any one remain who is willing to defend God? Berish declares:

> There is none—but who is to blame for that? His defenders? He killed them! He massacred His friends and allies! He could have spared Reb Shmuel the dayan, and Reb Yehuda Leib the cantor, and Reb Borukh the teacher, Hersh the sage, and Meilekh the shoemaker! He could have taken care of those who loved Him with all their hearts and believed in Him.

However, following upon much anguish and long debate, a stranger steps forward. The stranger, bearing the innocuous name of Sam, offers to defend God.

> I do not dispute the events, but I consider them to be highly irrelevant to the case before us, Your Honor. I do not deny that blood was shed and that life was extinguished, but I am asking the question: Who is to blame for all that? After all, the situation seems to me simple indeed: men and women and children were massacred by other men. Why involve, why implicate their Father in Heaven?...God is just, and His ways are just.... He created the world and me without asking for my opinion; He may do with both whatever He wishes. Our task is to glorify Him, to praise Him, to love Him—in spite of ourselves.

A resumption of the pogrom brings the play to a turbulent, ragged conclusion, but first a revelation is forthcoming. Who is this defender of God? Who would speak this way?

So—you took me for a saint, a Just? Me? How could you be that blind? How could you be that stupid? If you only knew, if you only knew.

Sam is revealed to be none other than Satan himself. And Satan is laughing.[7]

We are driven back to chapter 1 of this study, wherein the Devil is recognized as an expert in theodicy, the one who marshals a perfect justification of Evil: Himself.

III

Despite the irresolution at Shamgorod, or perhaps because of it, a sentence has to be handed down, if not by us then by other earthlings more faithful to the justice that is held to be divine. That sentence is tacit death, a living death, exile, a special Babylon for God Godself, where no songs are ever sung, no dancing ever done.

IV

If at Shamgorod (as elsewhere) the Devil laughs, is there no one left to shed tears?

An added functional-archetypal event is reported to us, this one in Elie Wiesel's *Ani Maamin: A Song Lost and Found Again,* a poetic re-telling of a Talmudic tale.[8]

There are remorseless intercessions and terrible denunciations of God by no less a post-*Shoah* trinity than Abraham, Isaac, and Jacob. Isaac declares:

> You pledged me clemency, charity, compassion—
> not for myself alone,
> But also for my descendants.
> Why give them to death?

> You made me climb, then descend
> Mount Moriah—
> Crushed and silent.
> I did not know, my Lord, I did not know
> It was to see my children,
> Old and young,
> Arrive in Majdanek.

The chorus sings:

> Death serves you
> And is served by you.

And the narrator observes:

> Even while they invoke and celebrate their faith, the three plaintiffs
> speak, speak, speak—and the Judge remains silent.
> Abraham grows angry, Isaac
> pleads, Jacob implores: God is silent.

The narrator further reports that "a voice is heard, surely the voice of an angel come to plead God's cause." The voice declares:

> The Master of the World
> Disposes of the world.
> His creatures
> Do their creator's bidding,
> Accept his laws
> Without a question.

Do we not hear echoes in this angel of a man called Sam?

Yet there comes a Nevertheless.

When Abraham snatches a little girl from before the machine guns and runs like the wind to save her, and she whispers to him weakly that she believes in him, "he does not, cannot, see that God for the first time, permits a tear to cloud his eyes."

When Isaac beholds the mad Dayan singing "of his ancient and lost faith, of "love of God and love of man," of "the coming of the Messiah," Isaac too "does not, cannot, see that for the second time a tear streams down God's somber countenance, a countenance more somber than before."

And when Jacob finds a death camp inmate declaiming that the Haggadah lies, that God will not come, that the wish to be in Jerusalem will never be granted, but that he will continue to recite the Haggadah as if he believes in it, and still await the prophet Elijah as he did long ago, even though Elijah disappoint him, Jacob too "does not, cannot, see that God, surprised by his people, weeps for the third time—and this time without restraint, and with—yes—love. He weeps over his creation—and perhaps over much more than his creation."[9]

V

I am obliged to report to you that at this place—with this secret of God—the original pages telling of God's life journey unaccountably break off, at least those that have been entrusted to me or that I have not foolishly mislaid. For the remainder of our time together, we shall combine some lessons deriving from God's life journey with additional sources and reflections.

But I see that I have failed to include a further bit of information from Shamgorod. What it was that Abraham, Isaac, and Jacob did not, could not, see has brought this item back to mind: The trial of God is set upon the Feast of Purim, a day when, as Berish the innkeeper and prosecutor remarks, "everything goes." Why would I almost repress that piece of information?

Notes

1. "Trying to Pray," in Howard Schwartz, compiler and editor, *Gabriel's Palace: Jewish Mystical Tales* (New York: Oxford University Press, 1993), 267, slightly emended; for source, see 355.
2. Geddes MacGregor, *Angels: Ministers of Grace* (New York: Paragon House, 1988), 51.
3. H. Richard Niebuhr, *Faith on Earth: An Inquiry into the Structure of Human Faith,* ed. Richard R. Niebuhr (New Haven and London: Yale University Press, 1989), 61.
4. Alfred North Whitehead, *Religion in the Making,* as cited in H. Richard Niebuhr, *Radical Monotheism and Western Culture* (New York: Harper & Bros., 1960), 123-24.
5. H. R. Niebuhr, *Radical Monotheism,* 125.
6. Elie Wiesel, *The Trial of God (as it was held on 25 February 1649, in Shamgorod),* a play in three acts, trans. Marion Wiesel (New York: Random House, 1979).
7. Ibid., 103-04, 128, 157, 161.
8. Elie Wiesel, *Ani Maamin: A Song Lost and Found Again,* trans. Marion Wiesel (New York: Random House, 1973).
9. Ibid., 17 ff., 31, 33, 49, 55, 65, 67, 89-103.

Part III

Long Though by No Means Lost Weekend

*Did the Goddess, in some secret laboratory of
vulnerable flesh, work out the mutations of the
AIDS virus . . . We are more ethical than God.
Given the power to make a world, we would never
have made this one.*
                                    —Catherine Madsen

*No statement, theological or otherwise, should be
made that would not be credible in the presence of
burning children. Any easy affirmation of God
would appear to mock the burning children. Any
easy denial of God would appear to turn the
children's deaths into a gigantic travesty. A simple
denial of God would appear to deny the reality of
redemption in our time and the validation of
biblical promise by contemporary fulfillment. How
can one speak of God with integrity?*
                                    —Irving Greenberg

*To submit blindly to God...would be to diminish
Him.... There remains laughter, metaphysical
laughter.*
                                    —Elie Wiesel

8

Comedy of Expiation?
Comedy of Redemption?

The storyteller must keep alive the most improbable flame, that of hope.

—Fernando Savater

[Why must she do that? How is she to do that?—A.R.E.]

What is to be the disposition of the pages we have assembled from the life journey of God?

Those pages are so fragmentary! They raise many questions. Yet perhaps we can build upon them, in part by exegesis, admittedly by eisegesis, withal by appropriating their wisdom. With the pages as guide, as teaching (torah? Torah?) we may be helped to benefit from further reflection.

These questions abide throughout as the really terrifying ones: How can there be an integral comedy of redemption apart from a moral condemnation of the divine for failing to satisfy God's own revealed standards of righteousness? And how can that comedy be complete until God actively atones for the infliction of radical evil and radical suffering?

I

For purposes of transition to this particular essay, I repeat two items from near the close of chapter 7: (a) We shared a secret that was being kept from Abraham, Isaac, and Jacob: the weeping of God; and (b) We were apprised that the trial of God at Shamgorod was set upon the Feast of Purim.

Are there special meanings in either or both of these data?

I saw somewhere that to qualify as truly *premier* the plot of a story ought to culminate in but a single major *dénouement*. I am unsure whether such singularity is a requisite for comic visions; I should rather wish that it is not. (Such visions do well to be more than a little mad.)

I am even being greedy enough to seek to untie the knot at no less than three places: (a) and (b) above, plus (c) a resolution (*dénouement*) consonant with the day *On the Way to Death* is being composed: Easter Monday. (From comments I have overheard some of you whispering to one another, few readers will be surprised to learn that the writing of this book will have taken no more than one measly day. But I have prepared a friendly riposte for you: Swift are the ways of divine inspiration—sometimes known as Godspeed.)

The long weekend that provides the title of part III of the book is meant to extend from Friday through the following Monday. I add two considerations to this.

First, an explanatory comment: The Friday–Sunday period primarily involves tasks that are assigned to God as chief protagonist in *On the Way to Death*, or that humans should desire God to take on (this chapter); the program for Easter Monday remains as primarily a human responsibility (chapter 9).

Second, a tantalizing observation, the full import of which will be disclosed only as chapters 8 and 9 come to fulfillment: Easter Monday is going to be espoused to Purim. This latter will suggest the way to a *rapprochement* between *dénouement* (a) and *dénouement* (c), namely, via *dénouement* (b). What have we said above concerning the desirability of a single *dénouement premier*? My insecurity is lessened a little through help from a particular candidate for that place: *The God that weeps and the Purim that laughs are met upon Easter Monday.* As for you, I beg for a bit of patience; all things are going to come out in the wash. As for me, I hope I haven't already let the cat too far out of the bag.

II

In the passage that follows, H. Richard Niebuhr provides an overview of the faith-cum-unfaith/unfaith-cum-faith of Christians (what I should call their deciduous love/hatred of God): "We are able to say in the midst of our vast distrust, our betraying and being betrayed, our certainty of death and our temptations to curse our birth: 'Abba, our Father.' And this we say to the Ground of Being, to the mystery out of which we come, to the power over our life and death. 'Our Father, who art in heaven, hallowed be they name' (Matt. 6:9-12; Luke 11:2-4). 'I believe, help thou mine unbelief' (Mark 9:24)."[1]

Christians distrust God, and with the foremost of reasons: In solidarity with others (many of whose suffering is even greater), they are betrayed and they are being betrayed. In solidarity with all of humanity and all of life, they never did ask to be born. And they are made certain of the terror of death. They believe in God, the Power that brings life. But they disbelieve (distrust) as well, for that Power also appears to end it all with death.

The question arising out of this condition is as elementary as it is inescapable: Does that Power, which we are forced at the ultimate reaches to link with death, therefore itself deserve to die? "A life for a life" or, better, one Life for countless lives.

The traditional Christian testimony has Jesus Christ dying "for" *human* sin. There is no need or wish here to obviate or even to temper that testimony. But will not an even more morally reliable judge—indeed, a higher moral jurisdiction—rule that the "death of God" is a just verdict before the fact of the *divine* sin? This latter issue is a million space/times removed from the question of whether humankind deserves to be punished for its transgressions, or deserves or does not deserve to be delivered from the terror of death. The real issue is whether a God that supports or makes possible that terror, together with other radical evil, *and does not (or, for that matter, cannot) do anything about it*, is worthy of respect, fealty, and worship—or is instead simply (NB) to be remanded to the diabolic, identified with the Devil.

What does God *do,* if God does anything? Is there reparation, is there expiation, for all our travail in the life we did not seek and for the prospect of death we find so hard to endure? Is there at least a divine comedy of some sort? Or is there only divine sin and therefore divine tragedy?

III

The long weekend gets under way on "Good Friday." The latter phrasing is incongruous (comical): Since when is the execution of a human being a "good" thing? That the expression is probably a corruption of

"God's Friday" brings little practical comfort, as long as we are prepared to receive as our own the truth of that day. To do this latter, we may replace "Good Friday" by calling up "Black Friday," a wording that no longer misleads.

Christians are sometimes heard to testify that upon the Cross the Lord "triumphed over the powers that opposed him." False. Jesus of Nazareth was victim—full stop. Jesus died. He was murdered. The context, the certainty, of the entire weekend is death.[2] If we expect to do comedy that makes some kind of sense, we had better be truthful. We had better face reality.

If in the presence of *this human being's* death, one desires a contrast that is authentic, there appears to be rather more hope for a tree:

> Though its root grows old in the earth,
> and its stump dies in the ground,
> yet at the scent of water it will bud
> and put forth branches like a young plant,
> But mortals die, and are laid low;
> humans expire, and where are they? (Job 14:8-10).

Well now, what do you know? No immortality for the human soul, as the Greeks vainly dreamed![3] No rebirth in the springtime with the crocus or the daffodil! "Mortals lie down and do not rise again" (Job 14:12a).

The context of our weekend is death. Is this to turn it into a weekend forever lost? Is death not only the context but also the *fabric* of these days?[4]

Why, for example, does there have to be a whole long day in between Black Friday and Easter Sunday? In *How To Tell God From the Devil* I offer one explanation: God couldn't stop laughing at Old Scratch, and this operated as a drag upon the divine efficiency. Another, but highly truistic accounting, is that the Sabbath (Saturday) is God's day off. A third possibility is that although God was fully prepared to put in overtime, the Devil proved more intransigent at the end than even God expected. But you may have an entirely different explanation.

The account that follows may or may not qualify for God's own pages; it is from a play by Rolf Hochhuth. Yet it is possessed of high relevance to our weekend, because in the act called "Auschwitz or The Question Asked of God" (the ultimate point of the drama, really) "The Doctor" is employing the instrument of murder and death in order to humiliate Father

Riccardo Fontana for his faith. In a reversal to the prologue of Job (wherein God permits Satan to test a singularly upright human individual), The Doctor is now testing God. Following upon Riccardo's question of why The Doctor is conducting this "boldest experiment," the other says:

> Because I wanted an answer—an answer!
> ...I risked what no man had
> yet risked since the world began to turn....
> I took an oath that I would provoke
> that old Man so measurelessly,
> so totally beyond measure, that he would have to
> give an answer.
> Even if it was only the negative answer, which
> as Stendahl says, is all that *can* excuse Him:
> that He does not exist.

Yet God has done nothing to respond or intervene. And so The Doctor goes on:

> Do you find it more comforting that God in person
> turns Mankind on the spit of history?...
> History: dust, altars, suffering, rape,
> where every reputation mocks its victims.
> Creator, creation, creature, all these three
> Auschwitz negates.

We are being compelled to choose: Is God truly unable to answer? Or is the test coming from the Devil? If the latter, then The Doctor's diabolism is what happens to human beings when they take part in this same kind of testing. Oddly enough—or is it odd?—The Doctor appears to opt for the second choice; he has already confessed that he is himself the Devil. (God is not the only One permitted an Incarnation; the Devil maintains that right as well.) And in a syllogism that would appeal to C. G. Jung, Jeffrey Burton Russell, and some of the rest of us, Riccardo cries out:

> If there is a Devil then there is a God:
> Or *you* would long ago have won.

But The Doctor only seizes Riccardo's arm and "bubbles with laughter":

> That's how I like to see you.
> The St. Vitus dance of the fanatic.[5]

Yet just who is the fanatic? And does God keep on being unable to answer?

All kinds of renderings and readings of the time between Friday and Sunday are possible, as you well know. From the human side, I prefer the name "Holy Saturday," though not so much because it is a day of holy warfare, but rather for another meaning of "holy": the uncertain, the unpredictable. Holy Saturday is that segment of the weekend when we are made to brood and wonder. For if God cannot raise God's own reputed Son from the dead, or (worse) can do so but fails to do it, then does not Death have a final say, and, to all intents and purposes, do not those rumors of God's own death (lifelessness) turn out to be true? A God with no power at all over Death might just as well be one more dead body floating down history's stream of corpses.

Or Death can gain an opposite meaning. "If mortals die, will they live again?" (Job 14:14).[6] The death of a mortal is an act of the Shadow (the Angel of Death in its devilish aspect); the resurrection of a mortal is an act of God stepping out from behind the Shadow (the Angel of Death in its godly aspect).

We may here be supplied with one rationale of Jesus' resurrection: Every once in a while God gets so *fed up* with the Devil (Godself) and his wanton behavior that God resolves to act—an instance of nothing but grace-filled self-immolation.

Another way to apprehend Jesus' death/resurrection is through a dialectic of "dark" vis-à-vis "light" comedy. In the former case, comedy is interpreted as destructive, morbid, perhaps demonic; in the latter case, comedy becomes creative, optimistic, perhaps even reasonable.[7] If God is to be unreservedly incarnate in a human person (a controversial declaration, to be sure), will not God have to die there?—since the one certain eschatological component of human existence is death. If the death of any human being is in essence a matter of comedy, that is, of the contradiction or absurdity of life, then the death of God-in-a-human-being is seen to be comedy in final form. But this latter does not have to be treated as "dark" comedy, insofar as it may be saying that God will not leave human beings lonely in their deaths but instead wills to share in them. Or—to go back to angelology—some of the angels may be conspiring to remind God that since humans never do ask to exist and surely do not ask to die, it would be well for God to stop fiddling around, get up on the heavenly horse, and cease forsaking the human creatures.

If you are interested (I have no idea what to do if you are not), I should like to make reference to one other interpretation of the resurrection, a special favorite of mine for three reasons: because of its help in coping with a certain ancient family quarrel, because of a willingness to stick its neck out in the theological-gender argument, and most of all because I wrote it:

> We are advised that the One who sits in the heavens is not above laughing certain parties to scorn (Ps. 2:4). What would be a better joke on those reactionary Sadducees [cf. Matt. 22:23; Mark 12:18] than for God to raise her own Pharisee-liberal Son from the dead! She would be having a go at one of her dearest truths, and would also be giving at least a few of her people a foretaste of the things that are to come. Maybe best of all, she would be reminding the Sadducees exactly what she thought of them, meanwhile assuring her good friends the Pharisees that she was on their side.[8]

End note: It is only Christians called Pollyanna (and equivalents) who perdure inside the Empty Tomb, not wishing to be reminded that, outside, the trial of God is still being held—not alone on 25 February 1649, but on uncounted other dates *post resurrectionem*.

IV

As we have been going along, I've had the feeling that the analysis can profit from additional literary exposition and criticism from within theology-as-comedy/theology-of-comedy (extending to issues of suffering and death). Our stress at this juncture upon *questions* of what the comedy of expiation and the comedy of redemption mean provides a good place for that kind of reporting, rumination, and assessment, and it bears as well upon the promise of Easter Monday (chapter 9). Let's think of the remainder of this eighth chapter as a serving of sample dialogues for special reflection upon Easter Day.

In his study *Theology as Comedy,* George Aichele, Jr. alludes to the conceit of many critics that "comedy refuses to take death seriously, because of its central message that life must and does endure." Against this presumption, Aichele calls to witness three creations: James Joyce's "The Dead," Samuel Beckett's *The Unnameable*, and Kurt Vonnegut's *Slaughterhouse-Five*. These sources support the contention that death can be "treated very seriously, without any diminution of the comic message. Indeed, it is precisely because death is seen as so final and so powerful that the comedy in these works becomes so crucial."[9]

In his essay on "The Possibilities of a Comic Theology," Aichele writes:

> Because comedy deals with the mundane, the lowly and ludicrous, the comic Christian thought must be that of humility: in its central and most explicit form, the humiliation of God become man.... Although the central image of this humility would be Jesus Christ, it would also take expression in numerous other ways—for example, in all the leaders, prophets, priests, apostles, disciples, and other "holy people" involved in the biblical stories. In these persons, the man suffers and his pride is humiliated before God, whereas in Jesus, it is God who gives himself to be humiliated by man. This theology sees atonement and salvation achieved by the mutual humiliation of man and God.

Humanity's sinful pride is such that it refuses divine help. "God must therefore humiliate himself to man; in so doing, he not only serves as the great example, but he actually participates in the reconciliation by providing the humility necessary to overcome all of man's pride." God takes "man's burden upon himself."[10]

Conspicuous and blessed enough in its presence here is atonement for humankind, a salvation for human beings made necessary by *human* sin. Just as conspicuous but now in its absence is the salvation that is necessary for God due to the *divine* sin. The atonement is, in effect, made into something anthropocentric, while God's own problem is, in effect, swept under the carpet. God condemns but then saves humanity; God does nothing to condemn or act to save Godself. There is divine humiliation, yet there is no divine self-humiliation. God has all kinds of compassion for humankind. But where is God's "compassion" for God's own integrity? Aichele speaks in behalf of a new Classicism in comedy, which includes *rationality,* the requirement *"that every factor be considered"* in contrast to the evil of partiality.[11] What a pity, therefore, that the one factor most in need of consideration, the divine transgression, is left out of consideration by Aichele. The "mutual humiliation" of which he speaks is focused upon the conquering of human pride and evil. The issue of human sin and forgiveness is helpfully and carefully addressed. But the issue of divine blameworthiness for radical human suffering and death is hopelessly lost.

In recent feminist thinking serious objections are raised against equating human sin with pride (contra Aichele). Anne E. Carr writes that "the Christian theology of sin as fundamentally pride, overriding self-esteem, or ambition is the result of a totally male-oriented set of reflections....

[The] experience of women is precisely the opposite. The 'sin' of women would more likely be characterized as a lack of pride, lack of self-esteem, lack of ambition or personal focus." Feminist thinkers "have shown how male theological perspectives have dominated understandings of sin as pride and rebellion against God and have failed to attend to the sin of those who are powerless, who lack agency, selfhood, and responsibility, who have suffered violence and abuse."[12]

However, while feminist theology has much to say about the suffering of God contra the old disgraceful (that is, devoid of grace) notion of impassibility,[13] that theology has not as yet contributed very much at the point of acknowledging and condemning the divine sinfulness. There is the severe sin of passively living with the divine sin and not doing anything about it. Surely an element within the struggle against powerlessness and in behalf of required human self-esteem is rejection of God's sin.

In alternate terminology, feminism's awareness of the Devil (objective, radical evil) is underdeveloped and weak. Judith Plaskow has pointed out that "feminists, although we continually confront human evil in the form of patriarchy and other destructive structures of hierarchical relation, have not yet fully addressed the theological question of evil as a feminist issue."[14] The stumbling block here is that "the theological question of evil" is as much, or more, a question of the divine culpability as/than it is a human "feminist issue"—or, for that matter, masculinist issue. The feminist insight into God as lover, friend, and companion, one who suffers and is compassionate[15]—in replacement of God as "dominating Other"[16]—does go a long way, and happily so, beyond old notions of divine impassibility and sovereignty, with puny, deviant humankind left as hardly anyone entitled to question God. The trouble is that feminist thinking tends to make God too "good" to be true, too good to be a sinner. Feminism's ability to recognize the Devil tends to be sabotaged by its too-rosy doctrine of God. Stress upon the male as working equivalent of the Devil (a viewpoint that is quite justified and centuries overdue) serves to get in the way of a necessary emphasis upon the divine blameworthiness and sin. This is highly ironic, since the Shadow of God remains a much more formidable and abiding adversary for women and the rest of us than does the male animal, however evil the latter assuredly is. What a pity it would be if feminism's entirely convincing realism about men and males were to become an (unknowing) companion to an entirely unconvincing idealism about God. As one female colleague has put it, while God may not be inherently evil, God does give evidence of being dangerous.[17] A comparably realistic note from within the feminist theology of God is sounded in Catherine Madsen's plaint that "If God Is God She Is Not Nice," along with five sympathetic responses to her essay.[18] Incidentally, one basis for not removing "he" and "him" from the Devil is its symbolic/moral reminder of especial evil that besets the male human and that the male manifests.[19] But should this seem to imply that the Shadow (cf. *animus*) has a proclivity to be male, while God as God (cf. *anima*) is better identified via the terms She, Her, etc., at least three firm responses are in order: "She" can be as much the bastard that "He" can be. Male humans share with female humans the singular innocence of never having "asked" to exist. But, as Patrick M. Arnold declares, "the dynamic feminine Age of Aquarius has begun, and nothing can or should be done to stop it."[20]

V

We move to another contemporary analyst.

The "central contention" of Ralph C. Wood's work upon Christian faith and comic vision is that "Jesus' death and resurrection render human existence comic in both its roots and its ramifications." In the "life, crucifixion, and final victory of Jesus" Christian faith "discerns a decisive turning for the whole of human history. The Place of the Skull, because sin and death have been conquered there, is the place past which there is no regression.... Because God in Christ has reconciled the world unto himself, we are no longer free to regard ourselves from a merely human point of view. The grim sobriety of the old aeon has been replaced with the gracious hilarity of God."[21]

Professor Wood has two problems. The first of these we have already met in George Aichele, Jr. How can there be human redemption in all its potential richness unless there is also God's own redemption? Whose "sin" is it that has been "conquered"? Wood gives no evidence of being aware that beyond the sin of humans stands the sin of the divine, which requires "reconciling unto" Godself and thereby unto humanity—a triumph over divine repression and hence over the evil Shadow.

The second problem may be intimated from Aichele's analysis dealt with above but it is nowhere made substantive there. This is the problem of the absolutism and supersessionism of traditional Christianity. In some contrast to Aichele, Wood extends his Christian conclusion to "human existence" as such, to "the whole of human history," to "the world" in its entirety. Even more ominously: it is the "grim sobriety of the old aeon" that is "replaced" by God's "hilarity."

Such old aeon/new aeon psychology and ideology sounds suspiciously and wearisomely familiar. Historically, Christian replacement theology of this kind has brought anything but comedy (joy) to those "outside" the fold. It has meant tragedy and suffering through the intolerance and oppression of Christendom.

The moral requirement for a veracious Christian comedy is made up of three necessary forms of atonement: for human sin, for the sin of God, and for special sins of Christians with their absolutist idolatries. Wood offers a slight hint of the right path to the third kind of accomplishment when he shifts from apologetic language to confessional language: "*We* can sport and dance like merry tumblers of the Lord because Christ is the Clown who has borne *our* griefs and carried *our* sorrows."[22] Here the good news for Christians *begins* to stop sounding like bad news for others. Authentic comedy is conducive to salvation; dogmatism is conducive to damnation. Good comedy is always watching its language.

Elsewhere Wood silences the note of supersessionism, as when he finds "Jews and Jesus," "Israel and Christ," equally proclaiming the divine grace in their place as one people of God.

> Faith...is the supremely comic act. It takes joy in the fact that God enjoys his people.... The central command and privilege of the faithful life is to dwell in gladness and trust rather than fear and distrust. Christians are enjoined, like liberated King David, to play and dance and sing before the ark of our redemption—rejoicing in the Lord always, becoming unabashed fools for Christ's sake.... It is unbelief that constitutes the ultimate lack of humor. Sin is the refusal to be cheered by God's unstinting largesse. It is the glum unwillingness to celebrate the divine comedy.[23]

With these words, the peril of Christian replacementism vis-à-vis Jews is avoided or is at least put in question. The issue stays, however, of what is to be the soteriological status of non-Christians and non-Jews in relation to the divine comedy. And, of course, the fundamental, all-decisive issue persists: If it is so that God can "enjoy his people," what then is God required to do in order that human beings, delivered from suffering and the terror of death, may "enjoy" God? Ralph C.

Wood's representation and sustained praise of Karl Barth as "theologian of the divine comedy," one whose theology "is characterized by an enormous gaiety," does not speak in any way to this issue. For Barth, God is Savior of all, of the world, the conqueror of human guilt. But who is going to save God?[24]

(I'm not sure I still have the stamina to reread Barth's massive volumes. I went entirely through him during those dear living days never beyond recall, and particularly over the course of a year at the University of Cambridge. I have a suspicion that Barth is the one responsible for making me so tired all the time. Gaiety-schmaiety.)

It is not accidental that Karl Barth should go out of his way to point out that the "Credo in diabolus" is not in the Christian creeds, but instead "Credo in Deus" is there.[25] Yet who has ever *claimed* that the Devil is an official article in Christian dogma? Doctrinal silence upon the Devil is precisely the Christian problem! The Devil may not be an article of traditional faith, but he is surely an article of objective truth, demonstrated over thousands of years by God's own creation and sustenance of evil (cf. Isa. 45:7). The Fourth Lateran Council, as cited in chapter seven, was entirely right in its insistence upon the reality of "Satan and the other devils," as proved by history past, history present, and, presumably, history future. Karl Barth is as much the theological dreamer as, or more a dreamer than, those few feminists referred to above. He even verges upon the logic of dualism.[26]

In the end Ralph C. Wood finds the "unique achievement" of Barth's theology to be the "joyous imbalance between humanity's sin and God's love.... The Christian proclamation is not, therefore, a message of joy *and* sadness. It is the comic announcement that the tragic duality and the sinful curse of human existence have been once and for all overcome.... God's decision is revealed in the Glad Tidings of our gracious acceptance despite our deserved rejection."[27]

Wood and Barth are at best half-correct. A message of joy is there all right in the (at least proleptic and eschatological) divine victory over human sin. But that message is counteracted by a message of sadness. For in both thinkers the trial of God is over, or, more accurately, no trial has ever been held. The divine culprit remains wholly at large. What about *God's* "deserved rejection"? In Barth as in unnumbered other Christian theologians and church people the Everest of immorality is scaled.

VI

Is the previous section of this chapter meant to imply that there may be no hope for Christianity, in light of its tacit hopelessness respecting any substantial readiness to come to terms with the divine sin, with God as Shadow? Is this the price that has to be paid for a quite justified stress upon human iniquity and upon God's graceful acts of atonement for that iniquity? Is it the case that Christian faith perforce allows, even encourages, the self-righteousness and arrogance of the Shadow of God to remain in power, effectively repressing the unrestricted self-humiliation and repentance of God? If so, the Christian comedy is decapitated.

The answer to the above questions is: No, not necessarily—and on a minimum of two grounds.

1. Even in the highly dubious thinking we have just reviewed, God is identified in terms that can conceivably open the door to actual divine self-repentance. These qualities include the humiliation of God, taking humankind's burdens upon Godself, and the divine suffering, grace, mercy, compassion, and love. For all the onesidedness and unrealism of the views we have just considered vis-à-vis the presence of radical evil, they just may help lead the way to an eventual acknowledgment *by God* of the Shadow as a living (deadly) manifestation of the divine self. Ralph C. Wood alludes to "the comic truth" as "unwittingly" attested to in the fiction of Peter De Vries: "Christ can take all the flung pies of human fury because he is the Clown who has borne our griefs and carried our sorrows, the Jester who is smitten of God, the Fool who, knowing no evil, was made sin that 'we might become the righteousness of God'" (II Cor. 5:21).[28] Ultimately, a God who is prepared to be Clown just may be able to make Godself ready to confess and atone for the divine sin. The "righteousness of God" may ultimately overtake the unrighteousness of the Shadow and cast it into outer darkness.

2. Within contemporary Christian theology itself signs have begun to appear of what we may call the higher morality of the divine blameworthiness, repentance, and atonement. Thus, for all his strictures against a traditional theism of divine omnipotence, Clark M. Williamson is still able to acknowledge as God's *"chief responsibility"* the bringing forth of "free and possibly uncooperative creatures."[29] Must not such divine responsibility carry with it culpability?

From within a few (as yet) available figures, we may concentrate upon one Christian theologian of the divine sin. Under the theme "The Utopianism of Job: From the Ethics of Obedience to the Ethics of Audacity," Darrell J. Fasching—in part following Jacques Ellul—applauds the *post-Shoah* insistence of Irving Greenberg, Emil Fackenheim, Elie Wiesel, Anson Laytner, and others upon a "uniquely Jewish narrative tradition" of chutzpa, a boldness respecting heaven (*hutzpa k'lapei shamaya*), a tradition that, as we have already seen, extends all the way back to Abraham.[30]

An essential caveat: We are to think of chutzpa, not as a questionable assertion of human willfulness or impudence (gall), but as an unqualifiedly rightful declaration of human dignity, grounded in the *imago dei,* and hence something that God Godself wishes for human beings. *Thus is chutzpa a materially holy act.*

Obedience to God is of course central for Judaism. But yet—so Fasching cites Anson Laytner—"there has existed alongside this mainstream tradition another expression of the covenantal relationship.... According to this view of the Covenant, it is as though God and the Jewish people grew up together and so treat each other with the familiarity common to old friends or lovers." It is this understanding of the divine-human relationship, with its emphasis upon divine as much as human obligation, that has made possible, as Fasching indicates, a theology of chutzpa. Mordechai Rotenberg identifies this form of audacity as "a symbol for man's capacity to affect God and to change his decrees and consequently man's future by his actions and justified complaints."[31]

Professor Fasching's exegesis of Job is apropos. No other biblical book represents the theme of faith as chutzpa "more profoundly than the Book of Job." Fasching notes a

> dialectical reversal of the trial metaphor. In the framing story (1-2:10 and 42:10-17) Job is put on trial by God, but in the main body of the book, the dialogue with the comforters, the roles of God and Job are reversed and Job places God on trial. The comforters wish to make Job guilty so that God does not appear unjust for allowing the infliction of suffering upon Job. Job refuses to play that game. He steadfastly insists: "Till I die I will not renounce my integrity. My innocence I maintain, I will not relinquish it" (27:5-6). So Job demands his day in court: "I will say to God: 'don't condemn me; let me know your case against me'" (10:2). Nevertheless he is skeptical that he will get a fair hearing: "But how can man be acquitted before God?...If I summoned and he answered, I do not believe he would heed me. He would crush me with a tempest" (9:2 and 9:16-17). Prophesying his

own fate that will come true when God finally appears to him in the whirlwind, still Job persists in his challenge: "Let Shaddai answer me" (31:35).

With the "comforters" of Job, a further dialectical reversal develops. For in the final chapter of the book God says to Eliphaz the Teminite: "My anger burns against you and your two friends; for you have not spoken truth of me, as did Job, my servant" (42:7). Fasching recounts as God's own confirmation that it was Job who "told the truth" while "the comforters were lying. The paradox is that Job is vindicated in his audacity to call the justice of God into question even though God must find God's own self guilty. God chooses to be on the side of human dignity and integrity even if it means that God's own authority must be called into question."[32]

I submit two critical midrashim: (1) Although Fasching alludes to God's answer to Job in chapters 38 ff., he does not permit this to offset his own argument. That God should place Job on trial does not enter substantively into Fasching's analysis; (2) I suggest that the effort of the biblical Job and his current spokesperson Darrell J. Fasching to call God to task—a calling that is possessed, to be sure, of unqualified moral legitimacy—is unfortunately obscured by treating God as the equivalent of a patsy. Here is high humor, even if unintended—humor in the form of preposterousness. Let us see how this is so.

In the exposition in chapter 6 of God's "pact" with Satan, as reported in Job 1, I propose that the notion of Job's blamelessness rests upon an impossible premise. There is no such thing as human innocence in the sense of sinlessness. Accordingly, the composer of Job would have been better advised, as I suggest in that earlier place, to have concentrated upon Job's having had no say in his birth. This would convey human innocence in its one and only valid form.

Thus, a second defect in the interpretation we have just reviewed is that God Godself is made to fall into the very same indefensible plight that one or another fallible or credulous human being falls into respecting Job's "sinlessness." This latter assertion is what (allegedly) forces God to lambaste Job's friends while attributing "truth" to Job.

Somehow I doubt that God could be that stupid. God would seem to be quite aware, not alone of God's own Fall, but also of the fall of humankind. (Unless God doesn't read God's Bible any more. Too much watching the Boob Tube, even in heaven?) The shift that is morally obligated of us from human blameworthiness to divine blameworthiness can readily be achieved without, in effect, making God ridiculously gullible before the self-righteous and self-centered protestations of human beings. The blameworthiness of God is to be grounded, instead, where it belongs: upon the fact of the divine creation of humanity without any consent from humanity. Here lies any and every human being's authentic claim to innocence.

However, the error upon Professor Fasching's part, together with the first error, proves to be very minor. It does nothing to affect the worth or significance of his contribution: to firm up a morally obligatory theology-of-chutzpa/ethic-of-audacity within Christian thinking of today. Fasching's application of this ethic centers and culminates in the acceptance of "the stranger":

> In the biblical tradition, one encounters God, as Jacob did, through the encounter with the *stranger*—the one who is alien or wholly other than oneself and one's religion or culture. Biblical ethics is grounded in the ability to identify with the stranger. The command to welcome the stranger appears more often (some thirty-six times) than any other command in the Tanakh (Old Testament). "You must not oppress the stranger; you know how a stranger feels, for you lived as strangers in the land of Egypt" (Exodus 23:9). Knowing how the stranger feels one must "Love the stranger, then, for you were strangers in the land of Egypt" (Deuteronomy 10:19). In encountering the stranger, one encounters a witness to the transcendence of God, one who, like God, cannot be domesticated to legitimate one's life or religion or cultural-national identity. Thus compassion for the stranger is an implicit recognition of the transcendence of God in the transcendent dignity of all persons [despite their sinfulness—A.R.E.]. Such compassion compels one to call into question all authority, sacred (i.e., the god of one's nation) or secular (i.e., the state), that would abuse the transcendent dignity.[33]

We emerge with the paradox-in-depth that nothing in God, not even the divine blameworthiness itself, can be licitly used against love of and justice for the neighbor any more than it can be used in support of the exaltation of one's own self-interest. The blameworthiness of God is to be endured by God alone, and it can only be redeemed by God. The "transcendent dignity" of God is thereby seen to be inseparable from the divine repentance, suffering, and self-redemption. The compassion of God and compassion for the neighbor are conjoined.

The demand to declare the divine blameworthiness and the demand to assert human dignity in an existence and a death humankind never chose for itself are brought together in such historically-decisive judgments as that of Darrell J. Fasching: The religious traditions are never able to explain why suffering is necessary in the first place.... The hunger of human beings for meaning is so great that we would rather believe we deserve to suffer than to believe the world is meaningless and unjust. But Auschwitz and Hiroshima are events of such devastating proportions that not only the "suffering for our sins" apologetic of the biblical traditions, but...the "bad karma" apologetic of the Asian traditions...[are merely inadequate and desperate] attempts to retain a hope that our world is a meaningful world. But both providence (i.e., belief in a just and merciful guiding presence in history) and karma (i.e., belief in cosmic justice over many life times) as myths of cosmic meaning are shattered on the rocks of Auschwitz and Hiroshima. Because of their unique narrative tradition of audacity, the *post-Shoah* Jewish theologians have become spokespersons for the whole human race.[34]

The death of a single innocent child from cancer or some other malignity is in fact sufficient to confirm Fasching's moral reasoning, even though such uniquely unique catastrophes as Auschwitz[35] and Hiroshima remain "sacred" to our memory of the unnumbered victims there (yet always at the moral risk that someone will come along and try to "explain" the events by trying [impossibly] to reduce them to a matter of human sin-and-freedom alone). In this connection, I propose that the *diabolic* is a more formidable, because more accurate and objectivist, category than the *demonic,* even if the two concepts are closely related in their ties to radical evil. Professor Fasching shows how the demonic emerges in human affairs in conjunction with certain psychological and social structures of human behavior and thinking.[36] While it is so that the results of demonic action are horrible, we must yet attest that, in contrast, the diabolic is a cosmic phenomenon, linked directly in one or another way to the divine itself. *Sine diabolo, nullus Deus.* Thus, while the demonic may be said to bring about unnumbered deaths and radical human suffering, the diabolic entails Death and Suffering in themselves. There is no comparison.

If the diabolic infinitely transcends the demonic, so too the divine act of atoning for the divine sin infinitely transcends the divine act of atoning for human sin. It is told that during the services of Rosh Hashana—of all times—Rebbe Levi-Yitzhak did not hesitate to remind God that God would have to ask forgiveness for the hardships God inflicted on the people of God. And thence "the plural of Yom Kippurim: the request for pardon is reciprocal."[37] Thus is it God Godself who atones for the diabolic, for the Devil, for the divine sin. Blessedly then, God is seen to be, not a mere politician, but a politician who subjects herself to righteousness. In truth, there is no holiness apart from righteousness: Isaiah 5:16.

Accordingly, with aid from a Christian acceptance—in thanksgiving to Jewish thinkers and the Jewish people—of a theology-of-chutzpa/ethic-of-audacity, it becomes possible to start to remove, or at least to live with, the question marks within the dual title to this chapter, "Comedy of Expiation? Comedy of Redemption?" Our sample dialogues for Easter Day have had a creative role to play. The question addressed to George Aichele, Jr. and to Ralph C. Wood, "How can there be human redemption in all its potential richness without God's own redemption?," begins to gain an answer, and an unflawed Christian comedy becomes possible. We seem to be hearing Elayne Boosler's voice once again: "Real comedy can't be learned; it comes from a need for justice." The meaning of Easter is expanded to include a divine suffering, death, and resurrection, not alone as a blessed response to human sin but as an infinitely more blessed response to the divine sin along with the special sins of Christians for their absolutist idolatries. Thus is fresh and new meaning given to the accounting of the eighth of our twenty-one divine adventures, "A Word from the Land of Syria": "Ephraim the Syrian constructed a dramatic dialogue in which Death, Gehenna, Sheol, and Satan all lament the death of Jesus, which they had hoped to use against God and humanity but which he cleverly turned against them." Because the last laugh of Jesus' death and resurrection is visited upon the Shadow of God (as well as upon human sin), it is also visited upon God Godself, with the whole made possible in and through the grace of God.

A true, fulfilled comedy of redemption extends to and indeed necessitates atonement for the divine sin. *O felix culpa dei!*

Epilogue: The climax to the archetypal act of Easter Sunday is the originating of Christianity reportedly by two women, Mary of Magdala "and the other Mary" (Matt. 28:1-8). Mark identifies "the other Mary" as the mother of James, and adds Salome to the group (16:1). Luke expands the company into Mary Magdalene, Joanna, Mary the mother of James, and "other women" (24:10). But John reduces the number back to just one: Mary Magdalene. By the merits of my love for Mary of Magdala, I cast my vote for John's version. In authentication of this love, I recently went on a pilgrimage with my wife Alice to Mary's tiny house. You can see it for yourself. It is just on the right side of the main road as you travel north from Tiberias. For years unending I have despised such horrors in John's Gospel as 8:44. Now, having been to Mary's home, I have come to feel a little less angry with John. Mary seems to be trying to reconcile us: Mary of Magdala, founder of the Christian faith. It is probably fitting, and a good lesson for any church tempted to be imperialist/arrogant/ supersessionist, that the home of its founder should remain so humble, even unvisited.

I have to include an ironic note. On Easter Day 1994—Mary's day— a number of Church of England priests were converted to Roman Catholicism.[38] Their prime beef? The ordination of women.

VII

The trial of God does not end, not even under the empowering aegis of Easter. But if the Shamgorod that is ever with us can take place as part of the Feast of Purim, so too may our long weekend—of despair, of brooding, of hope—gain its climax in Easter Monday.

Notes

1. H. Richard Niebuhr, *Faith on Earth: An Inquiry Into the Structure of Human Faith,* ed. Richard R. Niebuhr (New Haven and London: Yale University Press, 1989), 96–97.
2. A. Roy Eckardt, "If a Man Die, Is This a Death of God?," in *Collecting Myself: A Writer's Retrospective,* ed. Alice L. Eckardt (Atlanta: Scholars Press, 1993), 135.
3. Cf. Simon Wagstaff, the Space Wanderer, who "suffers from an old wound in his posterior and thus can't sit down long." On being asked how it feels to be ageless, he replies, "Immortality is a pain in the ass" (Kilgore Trout [Kurt Vonnegut, Jr.], *Venus on the Half-Shell* [New York: Dell Publishing Co., 1980], 7).
4. Eckardt, "If a Man Die," 136.
5. Rolf Hochhuth, *The Representative,* trans. Robert David MacDonald (London: Methuan & Co., 1963), Act V, Scene 2; see also Eckardt, "If a Man Die," 138–39. The German title of Hochhuth's *Der Stellvertreter* is better translated by *The Representative* than by, as in the American edition, *The Deputy.*
6. Eckardt, "If a Man Die," 136, 137.
7. Further to this distinction, see George Aichele, Jr., *Theology as Comedy: Critical and Theoretical Implications* (Lanham, Md.: University Press of America, 1980), 12 ff., 119, and passim.
8. A. Roy Eckardt, *For Righteousness' Sake* (Bloomington: Indiana University Press, 1987), 310. On Jesus and the Pharisees, consult, for example, Harvey Falk, *Jesus the Pharisee* (New York: Paulist Press, 1985); John T. Pawlikowski, *Christ in the Light of the Christian-Jewish Dialogue* (New York: Paulist Press, 1982); Leonard Swidler, *Yeshua* (Kansas City: Sheed and Ward, 1988); and Clark M. Williamson, *Has God Rejected His People?* (Nashville: Abingdon Press, 1982).
9. Aichele, *Theology as Comedy,* 43–55.
10. Ibid., 121, 122, 123.
11. Ibid., 134 (emphasis mine).

12. Anne E. Carr, *Transforming Grace: Christian Tradition and Women's Experience* (San Francisco: Harper & Row, 1988), 58, 186.

13. See, for example, Elizabeth A. Johnson, *She Who Is: The Mystery of God in Feminist Theological Discourse* (New York: Crossroad, 1993), 20–21, 246–48, 251–52; Isabel Carter Heyward, *The Redemption of God: A Theology of Mutual Relation* (Washington: University Press of America, 1982). Cf. *The Emptying God: A Buddhist-Jewish-Christian Conversation,* ed. John B. Cobb, Jr. and Christopher Ives (Maryknoll, N.Y.: Orbis Books, 1990).

14. Judith Plaskow, *Standing Again at Sinai: Judaism from a Feminist Perspective* (San Francisco: Harper & Row, 1990), 168.

15. See, for example, Wendy Farley's fine study, *Tragic Vision and Divine Compassion: A Contemporary Theodicy* (Louisville: Westminster/ John Knox Press, 1990).

16. Plaskow, *Standing Again at Sinai,* 128 ff.

17. Professor Chava Weissler of Lehigh University (personal conversation, 12 September 1993).

18. Catherine Madsen, "If God Is God She Is Not Nice," roundtable discussion together with Starhawk, Emily Culpepper, Arthur Waskow, Anne C. Klein, and Karen Baker-Fletcher, *Journal of Feminist Studies in Religion* 5 (Spring 1989): 103–17.

19. Consult A. Roy Eckardt, *Black-Woman-Jew: Three Wars for Human Liberation* (Bloomington: Indiana University Press, 1989), chaps. 8–12. In a review of the above volume, Julius Lester exemplifies maleist ideology (in the Marxian sense of collective self-interest) in his monstrous finding that it is downright "silly" of me to write of the dangers that women face from men (*Studies in Contemporary Jewry* 8 [1992]: 335). For good counterblows to Lester's maleist insufferableness, consult Patrick M. Arnold, *Wildmen, Warriors, and Kings: Masculine Spirituality and the Bible* (New York: Crossroad, 1991); Philip Culbertson, *New Adam: The Future of Male Spirituality* (Minneapolis: Fortress Press, 1992); and Dwight H. Judy, *Healing the Male Soul: Christianity and the Mythic Journey* (New York: Crossroad, 1992). Misandry is as great an evil as misogyny (Arnold, chap. 3). See ibid., 57–60, on the Gaialogians whose hate ideology has them making a male God inherently evil.

20. Arnold, *Wildmen,* ix.

21. Ralph C. Wood, *The Comedy of Redemption: Christian Faith and Comic Vision in Four American Novelists* (Notre Dame: University of Notre Dame Press, 1988), 1–2. The novelists referred to in the subtitle are Flannery O'Connor, Walker Percy, John Updike, and Peter De Vries. We are not here examining Wood's exposition of these writers (chaps. 5–12). For example, Flannery O'Connor at times suspends her characters between the practically equal powers of God and Satan. Again, Walker Percy attests that "the peace of God, it is no peace/But strife closed in the sod" (100, 137).

22. Wood, *Comedy of Redemption,* 22 (*emphasis mine*).

23. Ibid., 32.

24. Consult ibid., chaps. 2, 3, 12; 281–83. "The doctrine for which the stern John Calvin is most celebrated and castigated—the dread decree of election—becomes, in Barth, the basis for his theology of joy and celebration" (35; see also 36, 37).

25. Ibid., 39. Wood is not wholly uncritical respecting Barth's position on evil. Much of the latter's problem lies in, on the one hand, a tendency to reduce evil to human sin, and, on the other hand, a conception of evil as essentially unreal; see Wood,

37 ff. In this, Barth lands himself in the same impossible situation as Augustine and H. Richard Niebuhr (cf. A. Roy Eckardt, *How To Tell God From the Devil* [New Brunswick and London: Transaction Publishers, Rutgers University, 1995], chap. 4).

26. Karl Barth, *Church Dogmatics,* ed. G. W. Bromiley and T. F. Torrance (Edinburgh: T. and T. Clark, 1934-1969), III, 2, 616-17; III, 3, 296-97; Wood, *Comedy of Redemption,* 42-45.

27. Wood, *Comedy of Redemption,* 48, 281.

28. Ibid., 270.

29. Clark M. Williamson, *A Guest in the House of Israel: Post-Holocaust Church Theology* (Louisville: Westminster/John Knox Press, 1993), 202-24 (emphasis mine).

30. Consult also Belden C. Lane, "*Hutzpa K'Lapei Shamaya*: A Christian Response to the Jewish Tradition of Arguing With God," *Journal of Ecumenical Studies* 23 (1986): 567-86; particularly the section "The Absence of *Hutzpa* in Christian Prayer" (582-86).

31. Darrell J. Fasching, *The Ethical Challenge of Auschwitz and Hiroshima: Apocalypse or Utopia?* (Albany: State University of New York Press, 1993), 161-62; *Narrative Theology After Auschwitz: From Alienation to Ethics* (Minneapolis: Fortress Press, 1992), 51. The Anson Laytner citation is from *Arguing With God: A Jewish Tradition* (Northvale, N.J. and London: Jason Aronson, 1990), xvi, xvii; the Mordechai Rotenberg citation is from *Dialogue With Deviance: The Hasidic Ethic and a Theory of Social Construction* (Philadelphia: Institute for the Study of Human Issues, 1983), 14. In his study of "The Ninety-Three Beit-Ya'akov Martyrs: Towards the Making of a Historiosophy," Zev Garber equates chutzpa with "supreme self-confidence." Rather than submit to forced prostitution as demanded by German soldiers in August 1942, these Jewish maidens and their teacher took poison and died "in order to sanctify the Name of God by their death as well as by their lives" (*Shofar* 12 [Fall 1993]: 69-92).

32. Fasching, *Ethical Challenge,* 163-65. In fairness to Karl Barth, it must be said, in Ralph C. Wood's wording, that "Job is justified, Barth argues, not only as he repents in dust and ashes, but also as he rails against the God who proclaims himself merciful but seems altogether monstrous" (Wood, *Comedy of Redemption,* 269). Further to contemporary Jewish thinking, consult David J. Wolpe, *The Healer of Shattered Hearts* (New York: Henry Holt, 1990), 140-46, "God Is Guilty."

33. Fasching, *Ethical Challenge,* 167.

34. Ibid., 172-74. Fasching, rejecting any absolutizing of the Christian faith, speaks for a universal ethic of human rights and human dignity (ibid., 176-211). His slightly earlier study, *Narrative Theology After Auschwitz,* considers intensively a theology-of-chutzpa/ethic-of-audacity. Consult especially this other volume, chap. 5, "Reconstructing Christian Narrative Ethics."

35. There is, however, a horror in the *Shoah* that distinguishes its unique uniqueness from all other events, including Hiroshima and Nagasaki: the German Nazi resolve that not a single Jew be allowed to exist anywhere in the world. This was an absolute "first" in human history.

36. Fasching, *Ethical Challenge,* 92-93, 169. But see Fasching's exposition of "the abyss of the infinite and the abyss of the demonic" as "one and the same abyss" without, however, claiming a single source for the transcendent and the demonic;

ibid., 204–05. Consult also Fasching, "Demythologizing the Demonic," chap. 4 of *Narrative Theology*. Further to the demonic, consult Walter Wink, "The Demons," chap. 2 of *Unmasking the Powers* (Philadelphia: Fortress Press, 1986), and passim.

37. Elie Wiesel, *Souls on Fire: Portraits and Legends of Hasidic Masters*, trans. Marion Wiesel (New York: Vintage Books, 1973), 107.

38. As foretold by Tim Bradshaw in *The Times* (London) (29 January 1994).

9

The Easter Monday of the Imperfect Fool

The Devil...is a manifestation of the divine.
—Jeffrey Burton Russell

*In the early Greek Orthodox tradition, an
unusual custom developed.... On the day after
Easter clergy and laity would gather in the
sanctuary to tell stories, jokes and anecdotes.
The reason given was that this was the most
fitting way of celebrating the big joke that God
has pulled on Satan in the resurrection.*
—Conrad Hyers

While the preceding chapter (the Friday-through-Sunday time) primarily involves praxis that is morally demanded of God, Easter Monday directs us to human responsibilities. Is there an especially fitting post-Easter-Day mode of response to the divine praxis? In the latter connection you will recall a promise I made in the first main section of chapter eight: to link Easter Monday and Purim.

By way of transition from the one chapter to the other, we might fabricate a little message for Christians who stayed home from church on Easter:

There is no such thing as nonreligion. For no matter how we twist or turn, we are unable to escape the Creation. We strike it every minute of every day—perhaps most peculiarly in sleep, when our unconscious goes to work and may succeed in getting "in touch." During ordinary waking times, the contact may be more vivid, but let us not ignore the dream life.[1] All in all, nonreligion might be better known as unitarianism of the First Person of the Trinity. Every human being is caught by the Creation, held by the Creation, blessed by the Creation. St. Anthony

(251?-356?) once said, "My book is the nature of created things, and it is present, when I will, for me to read the words of God."[2] Anthony's piety was of course a highly conscious thing, but maybe God is not entirely dumb after all.

I

The epigraphs to this chapter together represent the two sides of the challenge before us. We cannot repeat too many times Jeffrey Burton Russell's watchword, encapsulating as it does the unqualified, unending blameworthiness of God for the reality of radical evil and suffering. Yet then, in and through a reference to Greek Orthodox tradition, Conrad Hyers alludes, on the one hand, to what is *for Christians* a counterbalancing, act of God vis-à-vis the divine sin, and, on the other hand, to certain appropriate, responding forms of behavior on the part of the Christian community. What I say here of God's action against the divine sin is not drawn directly from Professor Hyers, yet the force of the assertion is seen when we equate, as we must, the "big joke" upon Satan with a joke upon Godself in the person of the Shadow.

There are certain continuities and discontinuities between the "perfect" Christian fool whom John Saward has portrayed for us and a rather alternative, earlier understanding of a comic Christian fool. These continuities/discontinuities will help orient us to the spirit and the meaning of Easter Monday as I am venturing to structure that day.

Saward's study bears the complete title *Perfect Fools: Folly for Christ's Sake in Catholic and Orthodox Spirituality*. It tells the story of those in East and West who "have received from God the rare and terrible charism of holy folly." The "fool for Christ's sake" protests "any attempt to deprive the gospel of its cutting-edge by conforming it to the wisdom of the world."[3]

A number of distinctive elements characterize the holy folly of the Christian East (these elements came to spread westward): (1) *Christocentricity*—There is "participation in the Lord's poverty, mockery, humiliation, nakedness, and self-emptying," divine acts that eventuate in human redemption. (Down in fourteenth-century England, William Langland was to proclaim that Christ had won his "joust" against the Devil); (2) *Charisma*—Involved is "a vocation and gift from God," sharply distinguished from "simple eccentricity or pathological madness." "Byzantine Christianity was truly fascinated by the figure of the holy madman, the unruly misfit whose repellant aspect conceals a Christlike beauty";[4] (3) *Simulation*—The holy fools "*play* at being mad." The fool is "a sacred jester, clown, or mimic. He leads a double life: 'on stage' (in the streets, by day) he is imbecile; 'in private' (in church, at night) he is a man of prayer.... To the world, with its ungodly idea of sanity, the fools 'really' were mad; to God, they 'really' were wise." (Saward is fully cognizant of a different "madness caused by demonic possession, a 'folly for the sake of Satan'");[5] (4) *Eschatological discrimination*—"The holy fool proclaims the conflict between this present world and the world to come"; (5) *Pilgrimage*—The fool is a nomad who wanders in the wilderness, almost always a stranger or foreigner; (6) *The political factor*—The fool's power and influence depend upon his being "an unstable element" in an otherwise harmoniously knit society;[6] (7) *The discernment of spirits*—The fool "penetrates the facade of conventional respectability," denouncing pious hypocrisy, self-righteousness, and self-deception; (8) *Asceticism*—"The fool has 'gone out of his mind,' the mind obsessed with self, the mind 'set on the flesh' (Rom. 8:7); he has unlearnt the egotistical prudence of the world; he has exorcised Satan from his inner self." He is able, correspondingly, to identify "himself completely with the wretched of the earth." He lives with, serves, and shares the lot of beggars, lepers, prisoners, and mental and moral outcasts, always denouncing sin but unfailing in his love of sinners; (9)*Childlikeness*—Above all, the holy fool is protected by "purity and simplicity of heart."[7]

Under Saward's expert guidance, we are met subsequently by the praxis of the holy fools of Ireland, and thence are ushered into the golden age of the fools, sacred but also secular, beginning in the thirteenth century. In Francis of Assisi reside "all the elements of holy folly." But Saward identifies the sixteenth century as the fools' "finest hour," until they come to be "submerged beneath the cold, relentless sanity of the new age.... While medieval hagiographers delighted in the *hilaritas* of the saints, the English Puritans...regarded mirth as the product of human weakness, a consequence of the Fall." The "Calvinists saw only sin and degradation in the jester's art. Above all, they condemned what we have noted as one of the universal features of holy folly—the feigning of madness to conceal sanctity.... Man's natural play, delight, gladness of heart, feigned folly, have no equivalent or antitype in the [Puritan] kingdom of grace and stand condemned by God." (A problem Saward and like interpreters face, as we shall develop this, is that the perfect fools were hardly *playing* either; in point of fact, they went even farther toward graveness than the English Puritans.) Saward shows how the tradition of holy folly is carried ahead by Ignatius Loyola, Louis Lallamant, and the Jesuits and Carmelites, as by Benedict-Joseph Labre, a holy wanderer of eighteenth-century France and Italy, by Edward Bouverie Pusey in nineteenth-century Oxford, and, once again, by the fools of modern and even contemporary Ireland.[8]

In a concluding summary passage John Saward writes:

> If perfection requires us to take up our cross and follow Christ, this will mean appearing foolish in the eyes of the world, for "the word of the cross is folly to those who are perishing" (I Cor. 1:18). This primary, Pauline form of folly is incumbent upon all who seek perfection. There is, however, a second form of folly: some Christians are called a stage further, to be foolish in a particularly dramatic and symbolic way, not only in relation to the world but also, very often, in relation to the Church. This is the vocation of the fools for Christ's sake whose particular charism is to provoke and challenge their fellow Christians to remain faithful to folly in the first sense, the folly of the cross. We might, then, state this general rule: all saints are fools for Christ's sake, but some are called to be more foolish than others.[9]

II

The later lines of the foregoing citation prompt a sharp question: Are there not, or ought there not be, Christian fools who are called to be even more foolish than the "perfect fools"?—a further stage, a third form of folly.

Let us first acknowledge the continuities between perfect fool and this other kind of Christian fool. There is an easy sharing of elements 1–4, 6–7, and 9 in Saward's enumeration. Or at least our other fool will not object to these characteristics and attainments. Particularly, the other fool is unabashed in his representation of elements 1 and 9 (an ultimate dialectic). Perhaps lamentably, the other fool may tend to be a stay-at-home (cf. point 5), while yet sometimes seeming a stranger even to those near and dear. Myself? I have been a wanderer between the charming (and stubborn) Deutschiness of Upper Saucon Township, PA and the enduring (and stubborn) Medievalness of Oxford, UK. With respect to point 8, the other fool may well be both wine bibber and consumer of single-malt Scotch, together with roast beef and Yorkshire pudding, though his gluttony will be kept in check, if not by spiritual will power, then by the Specter of Cholesterol, the Menace of Fat.

So beside the perfect fool stands—how ought we name this other Christian?—*the imperfect fool.* The major discontinuity between the two is created by a gross deficiency in the piety of the perfect Christian fool. Accordingly, these even more foolish Christians will appear foolish, not alone in the eyes of the world, but probably the same way in the eyes of perfect fools (not to mention the eyes of the church).

The thesis to be developed, or (much less cautiously) the recognition that is prerequisite to any authentic redemption is that, theologically and morally, the perfection of the perfect fool is highly imperfect (because it is incomplete), whilst the perfection of the imperfect fool is perfect (because it attains completeness). For the issue we face is that of a needed *comprehensiveness of salvation,* the salvation of God as well as of humankind and of the rest of creation (including, as good Francis of Assisi teaches us, the very least and last insect). Here enters the folly of the cross in its eschatologically complete sense, for it now extends to the victory of God over Godself, thus making possible and encompassing God's own ultimate folly. Disappointing within the seemingly perfect fool is that fool's total and abject silence on the forbidden but sublime subject of the very redemption of the divine—and all, ironically enough, in the blessed name of humiliation. The poor perfect fool does not really know a humiliation that is final. Here is his real poverty. (Only the Devil, we remember, will agree to serve as defense attorney for God.)

We too may hold that the Christian fool will protest (in Saward's words) "any attempt to deprive the gospel of its cutting-edge by conforming it to the wisdom" of this world. But a fateful blunder intrudes. All unknowingly, the perfect fool—who is not only described but promoted by John Saward—is acting to "deprive the gospel of its cutting-edge" by restricting Christian truth to a wisdom that, while it knows full well the horrendous nature and power of human sin, utterly fails in its moral duty to reckon with the sin of God as Devil. The magnificent concentration of the perfect fool upon the divine atonement for human evil fills his cup to such overflowing that he is kept from a higher perfection: holy chutzpa, holy audacity. For, to him, attestation to the divine blameworthiness would be nothing less than blasphemy.

Saward makes the central affirmation of Christian faith to be "that God became man that man might become divine, that the perfect way to be human is to be divine, that the words of Jesus represent not an impossible dream but a pragmatic command: 'Be perfect, as your heavenly Father is perfect' (Matt. 5:19)."[10] What Saward and the perfect fools fail to provide is the other central affirmation that is available to Christian faith, an infinitely more blessed level of spirituality. To be wholly and "truly enraptured by the truth and glory of God"[11] is to know the penitence of God for the divine sin, the all-costly rejection by God of God's own evil Shadow. Accordingly, Saward's wording ought, *on the one hand,* stay exactly as he has it and, *on the other hand, in addition, and in all harmony and coherence,* read: "God became man that God might become wholly divine, that the perfect way to be divine is to confess One's own sin and to disown the Devil, and that the words of Jesus are to be supplemented (*not* replaced or contradicted) by the command, 'Be perfect, Heavenly Father/Mother, as you are already perfect in the apodictic moral demands of your own Torah, by dis-gracing your Shadow, with special reference to Death.'"

Again, the unrelenting seriousness with which perfect fools take themselves—the agony of their spirits—makes the English Puritans look like spiritual pikers. To run about naked as so many of the fools have been called to do (in honor of Christ's humiliation) would only be, in the Calvinist outlook, a scandalous betrayal of indispensable modesty. It is the terrible sobriety of the perfect fool (for all his attempts at gaiety and reputed openness to play) that explains how "in the Holy Orthodox Churches of the East 'fool for Christ's sake' is a hagiographical category like 'martyr,' 'virgin,' or 'confessor.'"[12] Accordingly, not too many perfect fools will be very comfortable with what is to go on in the local sanctuary on Easter Monday. Will not such proceedings be a waste of Christ's time? For prayers await, lepers and AIDS victims are to be hugged, and holy wanderings beckon. Notwithstanding, the good humor of the perfect fool[13] will be freed to become unreservedly ecstatic only when he is apprised and comes to believe that it is God's sins that are at stake and are on the way out. In the meantime, it is only the imperfect fool who is allowed to approximate a perfect clown. Her/his playfulness can be unbounded, her/his holy nonchalance unrestrained.

It is the special vocation of the imperfect fool to declare that God is now redeeming Godself by casting out the Devil. Such strivings as the perfect fool engages in day in and day out, the imperfect fool realizes on Easter Monday, though with revolutionist consequences for any and every day that follows. The endeavors of the imperfect fool hardly attain onto "the rare and terrible charism of holy folly" that John Saward and others celebrate in the holy fool. The imperfect fool makes no such claim for herself. There is little if any ground for anticipating that any imperfect fool will one day be canonized. Such "perfection" is absent here, for it has been made quite superfluous. The imperfect fool is not qualifying for personal sainthood, nor does she covet any such thing. She is called instead to a wholly (and holy) transpersonal task that is not conditioned by individual spiritual sanctity. The issue has nothing to do with the potential of human beings for charisma; it centers instead in the character of God: *Is God being saved*? The work of the perfect saint may make worldly mountains shake, but only the work of the imperfect fool can set the very galaxies and universes to trembling. Upon Easter Monday a fully comic posture can be achieved. Comedy becomes cosmic, the cosmic becomes comedic.

III

Can human abandon be utter—unqualifiedly so? Can human nonsense be untrammeled—unqualifiedly so? Can human joy be total— unqualifiedly so?

I hate to disappoint everybody—or somebody—but the answer to all such questions is No. As William James would have it, the skeleton is always "grinning in at the banquet." However, what people can do is to get themselves *ready* for the banquet: for such unqualified abandon, such unqualified nonsense, such unqualified joy. And that's what at least a few of them are enabled to do on Easter Monday. Some human beings will simply be acting out a myth that is pointing to the End. They will be having a little go at things proleptic.

And this is where Purim and Easter Monday are conjoined. If "paschal" appertains in one context to Passover and in another to Easter, so comedy appertains in one context to Purim and in another to Easter Monday.

Irving Greenberg sets the stage for Purim: This holiday celebrates yet admits "the narrow margin by which Jews snatched meaning from the jaws of tragedy and absurdity in history [cf. Black Friday—A.R.E.]. The humor, mockery, and tongue-in-cheek tone of the Book of Esther and of the holiday is a perfect way to express the ambiguities and reversals built into the occasion."

The holiday of Purim is marked not as "sacred time" but as a time of secularity and natural joy.... All men, women, and children are commanded to celebrate....

One has to love the Purim holiday. At what other time can one eat, drink (even get drunk!), send and receive gifts, make jokes and kid around...?

Still, the core religious model of Purim observance is the classic mode of reenactment. Jews relive the entire event, from the depths of despair and looming genocide to the delirious exaltation of deliverance, revenge, and victory....

...On this day, no fasting is permitted, no eulogies are given, no penitential prayers are recited. The Rabbis were so determined to make this point that they instructed people to drink—at least to the stage when they could no longer tell the difference between blessed Mordecai and cursed Haman. (Those who can't tell the difference all year long are excused on Purim.)

...Since on Purim the Jewish body was to be destroyed, the celebration must stuff the Jewish body for joy.

Greenberg concludes:

Humor expresses transcendence of unredeemed reality, and it takes sanctity itself with a sense of limits. Satire prevents us from making the sacred absolute (only God is absolute). [I should want to qualify this last to say that God is absolute when God liberates Godself from the Devil—A.R.E.].... If people take the sacred too solemnly, they are confusing their religious expression—which is relative and limited in truth—with the infinite God.... The humor is in part a defiance and an outcry.

...Purim is the balance to Passover; it is the humor that admits that the Shabbat is still a dream. To act as if Shabbat and the final redemption are fact would be insane; but not to affirm the totality of hope would be a sellout. Purim offers an alternative: humorous affirmation. Thus, Purim's laughter preserves integrity and sanity together. This is Purim's remarkable role in Jewish history.[14]

According to one Talmudic midrash, come the Messianic time all the holidays will pass—save for Purim. Purim alone will endure.[15]

Over inside the church of the imperfect fool, resonations of Purim ring out. All fasting and teetotaling are strictly forbidden. Cries of "deliverance, revenge, and victory" sound forth. The accompanying defiance is directed at the Shadow. Easter Monday is the balance to Black Friday; it is the comedy that admits that Easter Day is still a dream. That is to say, to affirm that Easter and the final redemption of all are fact "would be insane; but not to affirm the totality of hope would be a sellout." Easter Monday presents an alternative: comic affirmation. Thus does Easter Monday's laughter preserve "integrity and sanity together." This may be the remarkable role of Easter Monday in Christian history. Indeed, in the Reign of God all Christian holidays will pass, save for Easter Monday. Easter Monday alone will endure.

The corporate deliverance celebrated on Purim is wholly specific: from the Persians. So too is the deliverance of the Christian soul on Easter Monday: a deliverance, proleptically speaking, from Death itself.

IV

Before we are permitted to head out for the party, we must reckon with a final great impediment to having a good time there.

Who the hell are we to accuse God of, and punish God for, doing and sustaining evil? We are little nobodies. By contrast the perfect fool stands beyond reproach: His imitation of Jesus is pure. He is secure, while the imperfect fool remains pitiably vulnerable. The latter's vulnerability is not that of Jesus; it almost seems to be one of trying to take over the office of Jesus, the chutzpa of replacing Jesus, of committing the diabolic self-idolatry of appropriating (with enjoyment yet!) the charge that ought to remain exclusively the property of Jesus: "You have heard his blasphemy!" (Mark 14:64). Is not the imperfect fool ridden with a Messiah-complex? Does not the scenario read like a death wish gone bananas, a death wish turned upon its head? Maybe a real Messiah has the right to argue with God, but is it not his horrible strait that alone justifies this?: "My God, my God, why have you forsaken me?" (Matt. 27:46).

The blasphemy of the imperfect fool merits no such authentication. His blasphemy remains blasphemy, the reviling of God.

Unless...

We have been witnesses to remorseless denunciations of God by Abraham, Isaac, and Jacob, according to the tale *Ani Maamin* (chapter 7). But we have also been parties to a secret, a secret that is kept from all three patriarchs: the weeping of God. And then at the end we are told that God "weeps over his creation—and perhaps over *more than* his creation" (italics mine).

What is this *more*? I believe that an answer is available to us. The tears of God are shed for God's own sin, for the divine pact with Satan, for the terror of Death, for the suffering that is inflicted upon *this* child, *this* woman, *this* man, *this* lamb, *this* chipmunk, *this* bird. In chapter 8 we took notice of Rabbi Levi-Yitzhak's insistence upon the plural form Yom Kippurim, as demonstrating that the request for pardon must be reciprocal: of humankind from God, of God from humankind. But the question of questions is not whether we have the right to make accusations against God.

That issue is fairly easy to deal with. We do have such a right (cf., e.g., Gen. 18:25; Deut. 32:39; Job 3-41 passim; Isa. 5:16; 45:7; Jer. 20:14-18; I Cor. 15:26; Heb. 2:14; *The Trial of God; Ani Maamin*; Darrell J. Fasching and *hutzpa k'lapei shamaya*; and Patrick M. Arnold and his great and good masculinist plaint upon the dark side of God[16]). The question of questions is whether we also are being told to *forgive* God, a much more awesome deed. The challenge that confronts the imperfect fool (never the perfect fool; he doesn't even accuse God) is whether his pilgrimage is to mean going beyond accusation to forgiveness.

To forgive God is to enter into the ultimate, most absurd comic deed, beyond all perfect foolery: God is the one who is supposed to forgive us, stupid! No one has to be a perfect fool to know that.

All right: "Who is this that darkens counsel by words without knowledge? Where were we when God laid the foundations of the earth?" (as per Job 38:2, 4).

But, two things: (1) If Karl Barth wants me to acknowledge that it is not humankind's cosmos,[17] I am prepared to offer a deal (I am only a poor politician): Herr Doktor Barth, I will concede that it is *not* my cosmos, if you will be good enough to grant that it is *my* death; and (2) The human act that forgives God is not human at all, either in its source or its power. The *imitatio dei* enters. It is God forgiving God, as is God's right and no one else's. Thus can there be laughter—not at God, but with God. (Even the Devil—that *poor* Devil—never asked to be born.) In alternate wording: Only God can face off the Devil. Only God has the right to face off the Devil. And this is what the response of Easter Monday is all about. It is about grace. (Were Barth not so inconsistent with himself, he would appreciate this second point.)

It is past time to sum up: We are advised that in dying, Jesus is the victim of human sin. Who would wish to argue with that? The ordinary, nonbelieving longshoreman down at the local pub will go along: That poor sucker from Nazareth should never have been wasted like that. To stop with this point is not to be wrong, it is simply to end the story before it is finished. For if it is confessionally licit and even required to affirm that humans "are saved by God's weakness, poverty, humiliation and foolishness,"[18] how then is God to be saved? How is God to be made whole, freed of the Shadow, of the split of repression?

In two ways. First, via the divine repentance that journeys through the desert, traveling across the entire history of Israel and ending up upon a cross. Second, and in a diametrically opposite mode: by resurrection. For Jesus' death reveals him as well to be the victim of the divine sin. This is exactly what death is. Death is of the Devil, Shadow of God. So the very least that God ought to do is to raise Jesus from the dead. And that harvest is in truth reaped: "the first fruits of those who have died" (I Cor. 15:20). Here is the divine penitent at work all over again, the same One who weeps for Moses and all the others. Here are manifest, not weakness, poverty, humiliation, and foolishness, but proleptic power (grace), riches, self-assertion, and wisdom—all these in battle with, and victory over, the Shadow (Death, Evil, the Lie) that has been scarring the divine face so hideously. Yes, the trial of God must be held. The sentence demanded by the divine (devilish) crimes must be pronounced. Yet it is upon the Feast of Purim that the trial of God at Shamgorod is set. And that trial is set again, Christian imperfect-fool style, upon Easter Monday—in Dubuque and Capetown, Moscow and Liverpool, Buenos Aires and Copenhagen. Bear in mind, I entreat you, the date entered in this book's preface: Easter Monday, 4 April 1994.[19] The necessary punitiveness is lifted—for today is Purim/Easter Monday, when the foolishness of comedy reigns. Probably, it is well for God's soul that God keep in mind that the next time we may not be kidding (not every day is Easter Monday), just as it is well for us to remember the very same thing about God (not every day is Easter Sunday). All in all, the "unconditionality of God's mercy" (Ralph C. Wood) is not only an attribute of God; it is a demand placed upon God—by God.

The salvation of humans may help them smile a bit, but only the salvation of God can incarnate a *comedia essentia*. The prayer of God is actualized, "May it be my will that my mercy overcome my anger." There can be no Purim for the Devil, and no Easter Monday for him. On the day after Easter a few of us may start *living* with death—in dedication to the Clown Jesus, through whom the atonement of some humans is effectuated but through whom, and much more important, the atonement of the divine is also effectuated.

What a High Christology this character is sporting! (A final Joke?) But not, curiously and gladsomely enough, a Christology that has to offend Jews or anyone else. Let's hear it for *hutzpa k'lapei shamaya!*[20] Cool, man. Cool, woman. Cool, child.

I do have to remember that a Christology so high that it serves to redeem God as well as humans will seem, for many believers, to go right off the map and be totally out of its mind. Yet this is how, at last, we are readied—or I am—to take off for the party.

Notes

1. Consult the cover story in *Time* (29 November 1993): 46–59, on Freudian psychoanalysis and the issue of repression and the unconscious. See also Kelly Bulkeley, *The Wilderness of Dreams: Exploring the Religious Meaning of Dreams in Modern Western Culture* (Albany: State University of New York Press, 1993); Gayle Delaney, ed., *New Directions in Dream Interpretation* (Albany: State University of New York Press, 1993); and Alan Moffitt, Milton Kramer, and Robert Hoffmann, eds., *The Functions of Dreaming* (Albany: State University of New York Press, 1993).

2. Evagrius Ponticus, *Praktikos* xcii, trans. J. E. Bamberger, as cited in John Saward, *Perfect Fools: Folly for Christ's Sake in Catholic and Orthodox Spirituality* (Oxford: Oxford University Press, 1980), 42. Of much pertinence to my present study and interests is Bernhard W. Anderson, *Creation versus Chaos: The Reinterpretation of Mythical Symbolism in the Bible* (Philadelphia: Fortress Press, 1987).

3. Saward, *Perfect Fools*, ix, xi. Saward readily acknowledges that the holy fool is commonly found in many cultures and religions. The Russian Church retained the tradition of holy folly longer and more fervently than the Greeks. Thirty-six Russian fools have been canonized but just six Greeks (1, 21–22). Inversion in religion, wherein leaders and authority figures are ridiculed, is not limited to Judaism and Christianity; consult Mahadev L. Apte, *Humor and Laughter: An Anthropological Approach* (Ithaca and London: Cornell University Press, 1985), 155–61; more generally, chap. 5—"Humor in Religion." In a *festus fatuorum* (feast of fools), on or about 1 January, Friar Juniper, clown of the Franciscans, presided over the following: "Priests and clerks may be seen wearing masks and monstrous visages at the hours of office. They dance in the choir dressed as women, panders, or minstrels. They sing wanton songs. They eat black puddings at the horn of the altar while the celebrant is saying mass. They play at dice there. They cense with stinking smoke from the soles of old shoes. They run and leap through the church without a blush at their own shame. Finally they drive about the town and its theatre in shabby traps and carts; and roust the laughter of their fellows and the by-standers in infamous performances, with indecent gestures and verses scurrilous and unchaste!" (E. K. Chambers, *The Medieval Stage* (1903), 317, as cited in Norman N. Holland, *Laughing: A Psychology of Humor* [Ithaca and London: Cornell University Press, 1982], 39–40).

4. A distinctive case is the "holy madness" of the Cistercian Fathers with their "models or archetypes of Christian perfection": the child, the idiot, the pauper, the humiliated and infirm, the fool (ibid., 62; in general, chap. 5, "God's Jesters: The Cistercians").

5. For a twentieth-century representation of the latter, consult Malachi Martin, *Hostage to the Devil: The Possession and Exorcism of Five Living Americans* (San Francisco: HarperSanFrancisco, 1992).

6. Accordingly, where social stability and peace between church and state are disrupted, the fool tends to lose his special function.

7. Saward, *Perfect Fools*, 21, 25–30, 94.

8. Ibid., chaps. 3, 6; 84–87, 95–99, 101; chaps. 7–9, 11. Further to Francis of Assisi, consult Julien Green, *God's Fool: The Life and Times of Francis of Assisi,* trans. Peter Heinegg (San Francisco: Harper & Row, 1985).

9. Saward, *Perfect Fools,* 212.

10. Ibid.

11. Cf. ibid., 216.

12. Ibid., 12.

13. The greatest of the Irish fools radiated a lightness, mirth, gaiety, and joy—as did the eleventh-century hermits, particularly in Italy and France (ibid., 46 and chap. 4).

14. Irving Greenberg, *The Jewish Way: Living the Holidays* (New York: Summit Books, 1988), 237, 242, 243, 246, 247, 254, 257; on Purim overall, chap. 7.

15. Talmud *Yerushalmi Megillah* 1:5, cited in Irving Greenberg, *Guide to Purim* (New York: CLAL, National Jewish Conference Center, 1978), 20.

16. Patrick M. Arnold, *Wildmen, Warriors, and Kings: Masculine Spirituality and the Bible* (New York: Crossroad, 1991), 154–55.

17. Karl Barth, *Church Dogmatics,* ed. G. W. Bromiley and T. F. Torrance (Edinburgh: T. & T. Clark, 1934–1969), IV, 3, i, 431–32; Ralph C. Wood, *The Comedy of Redemption* (Notre Dame: University of Notre Dame Press, 1988), 269.

18. Saward, *Perfect Fools,* 62.

19. The year 1994 is a pretty appropriate one, what with Good Friday coming on 1 April. But, shucks, I see that I am three years too late for the really perfect year: 1991, when Easter Monday came on 1 April. And I doubt that I shall be around for the next such conjunction: 2013.

   Esther has been called the "book of the hiding God," since no reference is made to God therein. The present book may be hiding God too, but by the contrary method of referring to God a million times.

20. One could even argue, though we need not pursue the argument here, that the Jewish theology-of-chutzpa/ethic-of-audacity is in a sense "supersessionist" (i.e., morally/spiritually superior) vis-à-vis the much narrower and much less courageous Christian theology of the salvation of humankind alone, a theology quite wanting in the salvation of God.

10

How To Spend the Day After Easter

La littérature…c'est enfance enfin retrouvée.
—Georges Bataille

Humor is the protection of the holiness of God.
—Krister Stendahl

If for the Jew of Purim "everything goes" (as Berish the prosecutor puts it), so for Christians and their friends on Easter Monday eschatological laughter, even zaniness, becomes the order of the hour. In celebration of the (coming) salvation (wholeness) of humankind and the (coming) salvation (wholeness) of God, the imperfect fool goes cavorting all over the place, with various small children, kittens, puppies, colts, *et alii, ex aequo et bono,* tagging along behind.

Some of us, not very good at decking ourselves out in clown suits, may be able to make a few contributions of a verbal kind, foretastes of Delight, of a Realm where everything turns upside down (a Congruity that beats off all the incongruities, a God [Life] that is all in all). John Chrysostom said back in 390 C.E. that "it is not God who gives us the chance to play, but the Devil." Rather characteristically, Chrysostom had the whole thing ass-backwards.[1] As Conrad Hyers reverses Chrysostom, "it is not the Devil who gives us the chance to play, but God."[2] Yet nothing Pollyannalike is to go on here. Hyers continues that the authentic comic figure is "able to celebrate life not only when everything is coming up roses but when everything is coming up dandelions, or perhaps coming up nothing at all."[3] In that spirit, the pages immediately to follow are dedicated (a) to buffoons everywhere, from one who has been underachieving, and (b) to Jonah the Trickster.[4]

Note: I bear consummate blame for what takes shape here, including subheads, except where other names are indicated. There are three, not mutually exclusive ways to reckon with (that is, treat medically) the scatology that will pop up occasionally throughout the day's activities: (1) Observe the close linguistic affinity of "scatological" and "eschatological," and conclude that the klutz at work was actually thinking of heaven but somewhere along the way became a little confused; (2) Call upon orthodox Christian teaching and insist that since the creation is good (contra Gnostics, Manichees, and such like), any attempt to blue-pencil various excremental references—not to mention sexual ones—is a sign of heresy, of theological indecency; and (3) Rule that, when all is said and done, the offender is still a dirty old man.

How To Get Inside the Sanctuary
(For the Sake of Zeno and all Skeptics)

Outsider: We require a threshold, yes?
Insider: Why must we have a threshold?
Outsider: So that we can go from outside to inside.
Insider: That's not the problem.
Outsider: Nu? What *is* the problem?
Insider: Isn't the problem one of how to get to the threshold?
Outsider: I think we can handle that. Let's construct a threshold to the threshold.
Insider: It would be a great relief if that were the problem, but that's not the problem.
Outsider: Nu? What *is* the problem?
Insider: The problem is, how to get *there*—to the threshold of the threshold.
Outsider: You have a point. What we probably must do is to construct a threshold to the threshold to the threshold.
Insider: That's not the problem. What you do not seem to understand is that there can be no threshold at all, because there always has to be a threshold before that, and before that, and before that, *ad infinitum.*
Outsider: You convince me. You have made me a believer.
Insider: In that case, come inside before you freeze. Just step across that nonthreshold.

For Whom the Poll Tolls

As we enter the sanctuary we are each handed a copy of David Ellis Dickerson's creation, "How Ecumenical Are You?," and we are asked to share our answers with others in the course of the day-long party.

1. Purgatory is...
    a. like Hell, only nicer
    b. like Heaven, only worse

    c. like Limbo, only more interesting
2. Saint Augustine was...
    a. a bishop
    b. a hippo
    c. shaped a little like both
3. How do you pronounce "Augustine"?
    a. AW-gus-teen
    b. Ah-GUS-tin
    c. Depends on if you were raised Catholic or converted
4. The Apocrypha...
    a. is the only good reason to name your child Judith
    b. is still not a good reason to name your child Tobit
    c. makes memorizing the Bible that much more time-consuming
5. Which of the following people is most likely Protestant?
    a. Mary O'Shaugnessey
    b. Jesus Garcia
    c. Giuseppe Tattagia
    d. Anne-Marie LeBlank
    e. Jack Brown
6. If Catholics are Christians, why do they pray to Mary?
    a. tradition
    b. reverence
    c. You must be Protestant. Only a Protestant would ask that question.
7. Which of the following is not a Sacrament?
    a. marriage
    b. holy orders
    c. extreme unction
    d. confession
    e. Super Bowl Sunday
8. Genuflection...
    a. is less painful than kneeling
    b. burns more calories than meditation
    c. can be embarrassing for Protestants and dyslexics
9. The rhythm method...
    a. is hard to spell in your catechism book
    b. takes the fun out of monogamy
    c. was obviously not designed for white people
10. Which of the following statements is true about Heaven?
    a. The saints all hang out in the special Catholic section
    b. Protestants get in for free
    c. There aren't any stupid tests like this one

Scoring (in the celibate sense): Give yourself one point for every "a" answer, two points for every "b" answer, and three points for every "c" answer. Any time you got "d" or "e," give yourself as many points as you want, but we recommend not going higher than three (the number of the Trinity) or lower than one (the number of Popes, at least recently). Judge your knowledge of Catholicism based on the point chart below, which has been modified to accommodate ecumenical thinking:

25-30: GREAT JOB! Whether you're a Protestant or a Catholic, it's very clear that you answered mostly "c" answers.

15-24: HOORAY! You answered mostly "b" answers. This is no better or worse than what anybody else got.

10-14: AMAZING! It's clear that you answered mostly "a" answers, and that's as good as anything else. Celebrate by singing "Kum-Ba-Yah."

0-9: How the hell did you get less than ten points? What kind of moron are you?[5]

DIALOGUE WITH A BISHOP

Our master of ceremonies is Dr. Krister Stendahl of Harvard, Brandeis, and Points East. His welcoming remarks include this observation: "The intellectual is a person who sees problems where other people do not, and sees no problems where others see problems."[6] What with the huge crowd and all the confusion, it is hard to locate the individual who shouts an *éclaircissement* to this, but it may have been I: "A comic is a person who sees no problems where other people do not, and sees problems where others see problems." But since this may give an impression of selling the comic a bit short—no threats to anyone are allowed on Easter Monday—Stendahl and the respondent go on to agree: "The comic who is an intellectual sees and does not see problems where others see and do not see them." This brings sustained applause from two people. Only later do we learn that they are the only ones on hand who are neither comics nor intellectuals.

AMONG THOSE PRESENT

A few celebrities from show biz make their appearance (why should such poor souls as these be closed to salvation?). Here is a partial list:

Hoose Antler
Sir Desmond Behernigernernigen-Offagain
Heather Bitt
Bliss Bottomround
Joyboil Cant
James (Lefty) Foulbanks
Joan Hyacinth-Narcissus
Squandorot Leafwhistle
Hoizonard Malfeas
Almost Nobody (secretly a politician)
Soos Palindrome (author of *Bridge Over the River Trenchmouth*)
Sange Pijello
Ramapo Simmers
Runcible Spoon
Kim Unonoo-Jones

Exactly Seventeen Syllables
Or
You Are On Your Way into Outer Darkness

A good friend who does haiku has joined us: Jesa Near Bar. She consents to recite two of her creations.

Haiku to Time and Space
How can Buddha do
Wee-wee when not here?
Buddha
Not here is wee-wee.

Haiku to Pleasure
Use napkin with ice
Cream on stick. But swallow not
Napkin or wet stick.

Diabolic Definitions?[7]

Ambrose Beirce puts in a grudging appearance, by special permission of the Devil. He agrees to read several of his definitions.

Bacchus.	A convenient deity invented by the ancients as an excuse for getting drunk.
Baptism.	A sacred rite of such efficacy that he who finds himself in heaven without having undergone it will be unhappy forever.
Christian.	One who follows the teachings of Christ insofar as they are not inconsistent with a life of sin.[8]
Ghost.	The outward and visible sign of an inward fear.
I.	The first letter of the alphabet, the first word of the language, the first thought of the mind, the first object of affection.
Immoral.	Inexpedient.
Life.	A spiritual pickle preserving the body from decay.
Primate of England.	The Archbishop of Canterbury, who occupies Lambeth Palace when living and Westminster Abbey when dead. He is commonly dead.
War.	A byproduct of the arts of peace.
White.	Black.

Shedding the Past

One member of the congregation has at last gained U.S. citizenship. He recalls for us his experience upon first entering the country (17 July 1923).

Immigration inspector: Take off your phallus.
Would-be immigrant: I can't do that.

Immigration inspector: What do you mean, you can't do that? If I said, take off your coat, you would do it. The same goes for your phallus.

Would-be immigrant: I fully understand your instruction. But I can't take off my phallus.

Immigration inspector: Why not?

Would-be immigrant: It fell overboard.

Immigration inspector: No problem! Why didn't you say so in the beginning? Welcome to the United States of America!

BETWEEN YESTERDAY AND TOMORROW
OR
THE ADVENTURE OF THE SPECIOUS PRESENT

Alice and the Queen have stopped off for two spots of tea. Here is part of their conversation:

"It's very good jam," said the Queen.

"Well, I don't want any *to-day,* at any rate."

"You couldn't have it if you *did* want it," the Queen said. "The rule is jam to-morrow and jam yesterday—but never jam to-day."

"It *must* come sometimes to 'jam to-day,'" Alice objected.

"No, it can't," said the Queen. "It's jam every *other* day; to-day isn't any *other* day, you know."

"I don't understand you," said Alice. "It's dreadfully confusing."[9]

WITTGENSTEIN AND CARROLL

Following George Pitcher, John Allen Paulos cuts in—if everyone is welcome at the party, we can't very well exclude mathematicians—with a remark upon the interesting resemblance between the philosophic writings of Ludwig Wittgenstein and the work of Lewis Carroll.[10] Fantastically enough, Wittgenstein himself suddenly emerges from his state of occultation to shout over the hubbub and under the hubcaps: "The philosopher is the man who has to cure himself of many sicknesses of the understanding before he can arrive at the notions of a sound human understanding. If in the midst of life we are in death, so in sanity we are surrounded by madness."[11]

REPORT FROM GREENVILLE

On a not wholly dissimilar note, William H. Willimon of Duke University is kind enough to play for the assembly a tape of one of his recent telephone conversations, together with a little background explanation:

One of the hazards of serving a church in Greenville, South Carolina, is that one has to put up with the presence of Bob Jones University—"The World's Most Unusual University." When Bishop Tullis moved me to Greenville my friends said they would give me six months before I would be in hot water with the folks at Dr. Bob's school. In scarcely three months I had already had my first tiff with them over their dispute with the Internal Revenue Service. It seems that the I.R.S. wanted to take away Dr. Bob's tax exempt status because he had rules against interracial dating among his students. Ironically, I said that this was none of the I.R.S.'s business. It is not up to the tax people to judge what is a "valid religious belief." I simply said, in an interview with the *Greenville News,* that the I.R.S. ought to lay off the good Dr. Jones. "This is a free country," I said. "The Constitution guarantees that anybody can make a fool out of himself in the name of religion and get away with it. If Dr. Jones wants to give us Christians a bad name because of his racist attitudes, that's our problem, not the government's."

It seems that Dr. Jones was neither amused nor gratified by my support. In one of his evening chapel talks on his radio station he called me "a liar, a liberal, a Communist, and an apostate." That's gratitude for you. A few weeks later when Dr. Bob called upon the Lord to "smite Alexander Haig, hip and thigh," I decided not to have anything else to say about Dr. Jones or his racist school— he plays dirty.

One of my members, upon hearing that Dr. Jones had labeled me an "apostate" said, "We suspected our preacher of being a Democrat but I didn't know anything about him being an 'apostate.' Is that some kind of perversion?" With as little theology as we Methodists have to start with, it is tough for us to become apostates. At any rate, this was the setting of a telephone call which I received a week after Dr. Jones called me dirty names in a sermon.

HIM: "Hello, Dr. Willimon? This is Dean So-and-So of Bob Jones University. How are you tonight?"

ME: "Fine, at least I think I am."

HIM: "Good. Dr. Willimon, I was interested in your remarks about our school in the newspaper recently. I gathered, from reading your remarks, that you may not know much about our school. Perhaps you don't understand our programs, our goals."

ME: "Possibly. However, I was born in Greenville, lived here most of my life, so I have followed Dr. Jones and his machinations for many years. I may know more about him than you do."

HIM: "Well, er, uh, that may be but, Dr. Willimon, can we have a Christian-to-Christian talk?"

ME: "I can."

HIM: "Now Dr. Willimon, you believe in the Bible don't you?"

ME: "I certainly do."

HIM: "Of course. Well, Bob Jones University is founded and operated on strictly Biblical principles. Take, for instance, our policies on the mixing of the races."

ME: "Yes, let's take them."

HIM: "Well, they are based on strictly Biblical principles, on Biblical teaching."

ME: "I doubt that. I expect that they are based on Dr. Jones's personal opinions of what is right—as are many of your rules there."

HIM: "Now look here. (pause) Dr. Willimon, you have a family?"

ME: "Yes, I do."

HIM: "Do you have a daughter?" (At this point I knew what was coming. After all, I wasn't born and bred in South Carolina for nothing.)

ME: "I do."

HIM: "Well, how would you like for your own daughter to marry a black man?"

ME: "I wouldn't like it at all."

HIM: "Right, you wouldn't like it. Now, all our racial policies are trying to do is to support the very principles which you yourself believe in."

ME: "I wouldn't want my daughter to marry a *white* man. I wouldn't want her to marry *any* man. She is only five years old. Is Dr. Jones advocating little girls getting married to old men? I think that's sick. That's disgusting. Where does he get that out of the Bible? I think that's..."

HIM: "No, no. I meant that when she grows up, would you like her to marry a black man?"

ME: "Just the thought of it, my little, tiny daughter getting married. That's awful. Dr. Jones has some nerve calling *me* a Communist. I am going to condemn him from my pulpit next Sunday. It's a sin, a perversion! Little girls getting married before they even get a chance to be in kindergarten! It's an outrage!"

HIM: (Now shouting into the telephone.) "Would you listen to me! I am trying to tell you, if you'll just keep your mouth shut, that I was saying that, when your daughter got older, say twenty-five or so..."

ME: "Look, you stop talking about my daughter. You and Dr. Jones. Keep your hands off of her, you dirty old...."

HIM: "I can't believe that you are a minister of the Gospel. I can't believe that those people over at that church, even a *Methodist* church, put up with a preacher like you."

ME: "You've got your nerve calling me a disgrace. At least I'm not advocating all sorts of sexual perversions like you and Dr. Jones."

HIM: (Shouting even louder.) "I called you to have a Christian-to-Christian discussion. Are you trying to make fun of me?"

ME: "No, I'm trying to keep from crying over you."

HIM: "That does it. I don't have to take this!" (He slams down the receiver.)

Later the next week, on my way to work one morning, my car was hit in the rear by an older man who claimed that he was eating a banana and didn't see the light turn red. This seemed a reasonable explanation for why he crushed my bumper. We exchanged business cards. His card listed him as a professor of evangelism at Bob Jones University. It had a scripture quotation on the back of the card along with the slogan "Witnessing Is My Business."

For the time being I have sworn off having fun with the folk at Bob Jones. No more late night phone calls for me. They play rough. Not that they scare me, but I have a wife and two children to think about.[12]

Stringing Along

Charles Kuralt has come in from "the road" to report this little episode: "In Darwin, Minnesota, we spent a day with the owner of the world's largest ball of string. He kept adding to it while we talked. That's the trouble with owning the world's largest ball of string; you live in constant fear that somebody, somewhere, is making a larger ball of string."[13]

Everything's in a Name

One party goer has brought along a copy of the letters page of *The New York Times*. One letter is here reproduced without alteration:

To the Editor:
Further on "The Comic Books Break New Ground, Again" (editorial, Jan. 24), about Northstar, a Marvel Comics hero who has come out as gay: On April 6, 1941, Tarpé Mills, who had been working in the comic-book industry since 1938, created her most popular character, Miss Fury.
The character, originally called Black Fury, wore a black leopard-skin costume and battled gangsters, Nazi spies and crooked investigators. Although she possessed no special powers, her skill as a fighter made her a formidable opponent. With Miss Fury, Tarpé Mills reached beyond sexism to create an image of strength and integrity.
Comic books are most often seen as vehicles of escapism, but they can also focus on an issue. For example, Art Spiegelman's Maus series brings readers closer to Poland, before World War II and concentration camps, through a combination of words and images.
The assortment of comic books that is available ranges front the fantastical to the realistic. I am glad that characters like Miss Fury are still being created and facing new challenges.

PAOLA G. MUGGIA STUFF
Curator, Cartoon Art Museum
San Francisco, Jan. 25, 1992[14]

The Normality of Evil

Leonard Cohen has descended from Canada to share with us a few of his poems. Here is one (his title):

All There is to Know About Adolph Eichmann

EYES:..	Medium
HAIR:..	Medium
WEIGHT:..	Medium
HEIGHT:	Medium
DISTINGUISHING FEATURES:..................................	None
NUMBER OF FINGERS:	Ten

NUMBER OF TOES: .... Ten
INTELLIGENCE: .... Medium
What did you expect?
Talons?
Oversize incisors?
Green saliva?
Madness?[15]

UNRANDOM MOVEMENTS AT RANDOM HOUSE

An older, somewhat nonplussed-appearing congregant volunteers to read from *The Random House Dictionary of the English Language*. Following is the selection he chooses (slightly abridged but faithful to the original order):

scato—.	a learned borrowing from Greek meaning "excrement."
scatology.	the study of or preoccupation with excrement or obscenity.
scatoma.	a tumorlike mass of feces in the colon or rectum.
scatophagous.	coprophagous [feeding on dung, as certain beetles].
scatophagy.	the religious or pathological practice of eating excrement [A.R.E.: cf. Ezek. 4:15].
scatoscopy.	examination of the feces for diagnostic purposes.
scat singing.	singing in which the singer substitutes improvised nonsense syllables for the words of a song and tries to sound and phrase like a musical instrument.

LUPOWITZ AND THAT MISSING PERSON

I am so good as to read to the assembly my summary of Woody Allen's "Mr. Big":

A blonde model Heather Butkiss, really or not so really a Vassar student named Claire Rosensweig, asks private eye Kaiser Lupowitz to find a missing person, God. Claire has a philosophy paper due in January and she wants to *know* whereon she writes—none of that speculation stuff.

Lupowitz tries Rabbi Itzhak Wiseman but the rabbi is running scared, having been forbidden even to speak God's name. Lupowitz heads for Danny's Billiards over on Tenth Avenue. His immediate quarry is the forger Chicago Phil but Phil counsels that there's never been Anyone out there. "It's a void."

Claire has lied to Kaiser. It now appears that she goes to Radcliffe, but this does nothing to keep them from having a wild night together. Early the next morning Sergeant Reed calls to ask whether Considine—I mean Lupowitz—is still looking for God. Someone fitting God's description has just showed up at the morgue—D.O.A. [How else?—A.R.E.] They suspect an existentialist, because it is obviously a crime of passion. This points the finger at Lupowitz himself. He grabs a cab for Newark and Giordino's Italian Restaurant, where, in a back room, he finds His Holiness the Pope, sitting with two goons. The Pope offers him some fettucine. "God does exist?," Lupowitz ventures. Everyone breaks up. One hood says, "Oh, that's funny. Bright boy wants to know if He exists." Fittingly, the Pope makes the astounding revelation that Claire Rosenzweig is actually a professor of physics at Bryn Mawr.

Lupowitz does some fast checking, goes to Claire's apartment, and confronts her, Doctor Ellen Shepherd, the real culprit. It seems that Ellen's jazz musician boy-friend is into *believing* in God, while she wants *certainty*. And her mistake has been to trust Martin Buber, for he turns out to believe rather than to know, so she is left with no choice but to waste God. And now, before the professor can get Cowenhoven—I mean Lupowitz—with her forty-five, he drops her with his thirty-eight. In her death throes he manages to get her to understand: "The manifestation of the universe as a complex idea unto itself as opposed to being in or outside the true Being of itself is inherently a conceptual nothingness or Nothingness in relation to any abstract form of existing or to exist or having existed in perpetuity and not subject to laws of physicality or motion or ideas relating to non-matter or the lack of objective Being or subjective otherness."[16]

Having been made heady, not to mention footy, by my hit with the guests, via Woody Allen, I completely lose control and go on to bombard them with a whole congeries of congeries. But I can still operate alphabetically.

BE A LITTLE PATIENT

Catherine Emmerich, a nineteenth-century mystic, who had visions of the Devil, maintained that he would be dominant from 1970 to about 2000 but would then be chained. Let's all do our best to hang around for a few more years.

BREAKTHROUGH OUT OF INSIDE MONGOLIA

A great International Philosophy Conference is being held, somewhere in the Inner East, with scholars in attendance from the entire inhabited universe.

Long and arduous thought is given to the conference theme, "When is a man like a woman?" After seventeen years on that question, the conference remains hopelessly deadlocked, even gridlocked. Many delegates are packing to return home.

Suddenly, the Sage of Momindowee-pp, Inside Mongolia shouts to all in earshot: "When a man sits down to do doo-doo...." His words are interrupted and greeted with total derision. Huge rocks are thrown at the Sage of Momindowee-pp. Loud curses ring out. All agree, "We did not come all that distance to have to listen to this sort of nonsense!"

But the Sage persists, and continues "... because when a man sits to do doo-doo, he is also sitting down to do wee-wee."

A tremendous hush falls upon the assembly. At once, cheering breaks out. Shouts of "Bravo" are heard. Soon the Sage of Momindowee-pp is lifted on the shoulders of the crowd and carried around the coliseum amidst a great celebration.

The conference has gone down as one of the most significant, not alone in the history of philosophy, but even in the history of the history of philosophy.

THE CANADIAN WHO WENT FROM BEING A COCKALORUM
TO
A CONDITION OF COCK-A-HOOP

cockalorum. a self-important, pretentious little man.
cock-a-hoop. in a state of unrestrained joy and exultation.

CREEPY THINGS

inchworm. a baby footworm, q.v.
footworm. a baby yardworm, q.v.
yardworm. a friendly worm who lives in your garden.

ECLECTICISM IN ART

The trouble with oil paints is the more you mix the different colors together, the more you come out with vomit green.

FROM PEW TO PEW

Hattie: Does your cousin Alphonse have sexual organs?
Mattie: I wouldn't say that.
Hattie: Why do you speak this way?
Mattie: What could be sexual about an individual's pancreas, or liver, or ears?
Hattie: What about some of Alphonse's other organs?
Mattie: Well, I suppose his phallus is sexual—and of course his right lung.

GOURMET AT THE ESCHATON

'Midst one last taste of seven-grain bread
There comes a lambaste from seven-sin dread.

Upon the chew of this jellied biscuit
Spreds the chill word of ipse dixit.

Upon the joy of this creamy scone
There sounds the grim knell of Now, Begone.

'Midst sensate bliss from one more crumpet
Is heard the kiss of final trumpet.

HUDSON RIVER LEGACY

Credit my Aunt Fragile with making anorexia nervosa delectable. Every day for 42 years, during her commute to and fro on the Hoboken-Manhattan ferry, she would throw up, although always over the rail.

At last her fantasy would become reality. In 1988 she was hailed as Role Model of legions of younger women, from New Jersey as well as New York.

The irony is that throughout her life, my Aunt Fragile ate like a Pig. Her emesis perennis simply came from being seasick.

IN MEMORY OF C. G. J.

In the village of Betselzeugia a small child will all of a sudden whip out an archetype and mount it on his left sleeve to the delight of the tourists.

THE MYSTERIOUS EAST

The Nirvana Sutra?
This is last in line for cremation.
—Chen Lung-Hsin

ON THE NATURE OF TIME

Both the prospect and the retrospect of a journey or experience can be so enjoyable—much more so than the spect.
Why is that?

THE NEW TRINITARIANISM

Beginning January 1, 2000, by Vatican decree, the sign of the cross is to include this wording:

Father Fat Free
Son Fat Free
Holy Ghost Fat Free

ORAL HISTORY

What do Johnson & Johnson do once they have waxed their dental floss?
They wane.

OVERHEARD IN THE CHURCH MEN'S ROOM
OR
THREE CHEERS FOR THE BELGIANS

DISCIPLE TO SAGE: Can a man ever finish doing his wee-pee?[17]
SAGE TO DISCIPLE: He may reach what he thinks is the last drop...
DISCIPLE TO SAGE: Yes! Yes!
SAGE TO DISCIPLE: ...but the last drop is always followed by a drip.
DISCIPLE TO SAGE: Brilliant! Brilliant! Now would you be so kind, Blessed Master, to formulate for us out of your endless grace the General Principle grounded upon this form of experience?
SAGE TO DISCIPLE: Certainly, my son. It is not the drop but the drip of which Eternity is composed.

THE PHILOSOPHER AT WORK

He thought for a moment, all the while walloping his trallop.

A PROOF (AT LEAST 86%[18]) OF THE SINGULARITY OF GOD

Question: How do we know that there is only one God, and not two, three, or four?
Answer: Because, stupid, there is no Scotch like single-malt Scotch.

SELECTIONS FROM A POSTMODERNIST DICTIONARY

body English.	body language with a very peculiar accent.
chicken wire.	a device used by fowl to keep out rabbits and foxes.
éclaircissement.	a very rich French pastry.
impious.	a very short and mischievous pope who couldn't care less about religion.
indenture.	a medieval punch in the mouth.
magazine.	a cache of explosives that won't blow up provided you turn its pages with great care.
mealy-mouth.	the normal condition of a mealybug's mouth.
Mississippi.	hatred of a Sissippi, probably for being a Yankee.
monarch.	half human, half butterfly.
monkeyshines.	a primate's (bishop's) illegally produced whiskys (whiskeys).
ostracize.	telling the other bird to keep his head out of your sand.
pilgarlic.	a man who treats his head with a particularly smelly medication.
present.	a gift. Cf. *past.* a gift given yesterday; and *future.* a gift to be given tomorrow.
rectal.	a recital from which I has been thrown out.
summer squash.	a vegetative game you are not allowed to play in cold weather.
taxidermy.	a public vehicle that travels along anybody's skin.
termite.	a freshman who lasts only one semester.
theologian.	an ologian who has somehow made it to the top.
vanishing cream.	an unguent used by rabbits named Harvey.
whimsical.	ice cream that plays tricks on the stick.

THE SLIGHT REVENGE OF RUDOLF HEMMISH, CONGREGATION OFFICIAL

My temperature had plummeted to 48, I had no pulse, all vital signs were gone. The Man of Importance (1/3 Priest, 1/3 Minister, 1/3 Rabbi) was hovering over me, ecstatically readying himself for the disposal of his old enemy's remains.

In a flash, from between dying lips I wafted a huge wad of decaying Licorice Dumpling up at him, exploding it all over his fat face.

If that was not the surprise of his life, my name is not Xerxes Zerkzies.

However, since my name is not Xerxes Zerkzies, but F. Trylock Hanssch, a.k.a. Rudolf Hemmish, perhaps the Man of Importance was not so surprised after all.

THE SPIRITUAL LIFE

A converted cannibal is one who, on Friday, eats only fishermen.
—Emily Lotney

VARIETIES OF LASH

backlash.	special protection for people with eyes at the other end of the head.

students' eyelash.   a condition where pupil strikes pupil.
whiplash.   a small hair caught in the cream.

WAIST WATCH

Having first earned a white belt, Claridge was later awarded a black belt.
Not in Judo. In racism.
Claridge himself is a very light green.

THE SAGA OF SANDOR NEEDLEMAN

Woody Allen has joined the festivities, and proves to be the only one able to quiet me.

Allen has come directly from the cremation of Sandor Needleman; in fact he it was
who brought the marshmallows. He relates that Needleman's contribution to theodicy
was to teach that true evil "was only possible if its perpetrator was named Blackie or
Pete." Needleman's favorite saying was, "God is silent; now if we can only get Man to
shut up."

Sandor Needleman was cremated with his hat on—probably a first.[19]

ONE GRAND LADY

Geza Vermes of the University of Oxford has come along to read for us some poems
by his late wife Pamela. (Please allow the *possibility* of the following: the greater the
incongruity, the greater the comedy.) Here are two of the poems:

Hello Hello

hello hello
you dot on my table top
you infinitesimal
microscopical
insect person
you minuscule
animalcule
you very vulnerable
nearly invisible
insect person
hello hello

can it be
that (with respect)
almost nothing as you are
you carry a spark of the *Shekhinah*?

With You

peering ahead
into the pithy depths of deadness
where I'll not be

where I'll not be me
where I'll not be me with you
where I'll not be with my greatly loved
whom I may no longer see

peering ahead into the pitchy depths
where being perhaps with Him
I'll nevertheless no longer be me
no longer be me with you
how shall I not express
reverential happiness
for your being with me now
for my being with you now
o lovely lovely world

bearing in mind the day
when I may possibly be with Him
I notwithstanding clap my hands
ten thousand times
for presently being with you
for presently being with you[20]

In the End, Praise

Whether an Easter Monday party will best end in a contemporary prayer or in pure
playfulness is a moot question. Since he is a bishop, Dr. Stendahl quite naturally offers
a historical compromise. It consists in Giovanni Francesco Bernadone's Canticle of
Brother Sun, one version of which is in large measure here reproduced. For my part, it
is impossible to resist the mischievous sin of taking the witness of such a perfect fool
as St. Francis and applying it in the service of imperfect foolery. However, there is
evidence that Francis, who is not always serious about himself, might have a certain
empathy for the imperfect fool—not to mention for the imperfect fool's bent toward
panentheism.

Be praised, my Lord, for all your creatures.
In the first place for the blessed Brother Sun
who gives us the day and enlightens us through you.
He is beautiful and radiant with his great splendor,
Giving witness of you, most Omnipotent One.
Be praised, my Lord, for Sister Moon and the stars
Formed by you so bright, precious, and beautiful....
Be praised, my Lord, for Sister Water
So necessary yet so humble, precious, and chaste.[21]
Be praised, my Lord, for Brother Fire,
Who lights up the night,
He is beautiful and carefree, robust and fierce.
Be praised, my Lord, for our sister, Mother Earth,

who nourishes and watches us....
Be praised, my Lord, for those who pardon through your love
And bear weakness and trial.
Blessed are those who endure in peace,
For they will be crowned by you, Most High.
Be praised, my Lord, for our sister, Bodily Death,
Whom no living man can escape.
Woe to those who die in sin.
Blessed are those who discover thy holy will.
The second death will do them no harm.
Praise and bless the Lord.
Render him thanks.
Serve him with great humility. Amen.[22]

Notes

1. Consider Chrysostom's antisemitism.
2. Conrad Hyers, *And God Created Laughter: The Bible as Divine Comedy* (Atlanta: John Knox Press, 1987), 27.
3. Ibid., 35.
4. For an inimitable account, see Patrick M. Arnold, "Jonah the Trickster," in *Wildmen, Warriors, and Kings: Masculine Spirituality and the Bible* (New York: Crossroad, 1991).
5. David Ellis Dickerson, "How Ecumenical Are You?: A Quiz About Catholicism Especially For Protestants," *The Door* #118 (July/August 1991): 5.
6. A.R.E. first heard this finding of Bishop Stendahl at Wolfson College, Oxford on 3 May 1990. Krister Stendahl is no stranger to the world of Christian comedy. See, for example, his contributions in the Walter Pope Binn's Lecture Series (Liberty, Miss.: William Jewell College, 1987): "The Jewish Humor of Jesus," "Worship with Humor," and "Theology with Humor."
7. These definitions are adapted from Ambrose Bierce, *The Devil's Dictionary* (New York: Dover Publications, 1958). Party goers are left to decide for themselves which items are devilish and which are divine.
8. From the same Devil's standpoint, we may perhaps add that a Christian is a person who advocates the divine sin.
9. Lewis Carroll, *Through the Looking Glass,* as cited in John Allen Paulos, *Mathematics and Humor* (Chicago and London: University of Chicago Press, 1982), 68.
10. Paulos, *Mathematics,* 67–70. This may sound like the sort of finding we encounter in Woody Allen, but it happens to be veritable. The original George Pitcher essay is "Wittgenstein, Nonsense, and Lewis Carroll," *Massachusetts Review* (August 1966): 591–611, as alluded to by Paulos.
11. Ludwig Wittgenstein, as cited in Paulos, *Mathematics,* 70. Paulos puts in the one existentialist pot Woody Allen, Søren Kierkegaard, and Samuel Beckett.
12. William H. Willimon, compiler, *Last Laugh* (Nashville: Abingdon Press, 1991), 46–50.
13. Charles Kuralt, *A Life on the Road* (New York: G. P. Putnam's Sons, 1990), 146.

14. *The New York Times* (14 February 1992).

15. Leonard Cohen, *Stranger Music: Selected Poems and Songs* (New York: Pantheon Books, 1993), 53.

16. Summarized and adapted from Woody Allen, "Mr. Big," *Getting Even* (New York: Quality Paperback Book Club, 1989), 139-51. For a fine study see Graham McCann, *Woody Allen: New Yorker* (Cambridge: Polity Press, 1990).

17. Everyone knows that our country is on the verge of civil war—between parents who teach their little ones to say "wee-wee" and parents who insist on "pee-pee." No such strife could ever occur in Belgium, because "in Brussels there is the famous Manneken-Pis statue of a mere child doing a wee pee on nobody at all" (The Drunkards," in Maurice Carr, ed., *Waiter, There is [a] Fly in My Orange Juice* [Jerusalem: Shikmona Pub. Co., 1975], 219.)

18. The proof of the whisky (whiskey) is in the drinking but is also listed right there on the bottle.

19. Woody Allen, "Remembering Needleman," *Side Effects* (New York: Quality Paperbook Book Club, 1989), 4, 5, 8.

20. Pamela Vermes, *The Riddle of the Sparks* (Oxford: Foxcombe Press, 1993), 36, 58.

21. St. Francis did not live in the American Middlewest in, for example, the Summer of 1993 or he probably would have spoken quite differently. The Missouri and Mississippi rivers could hardly be accused of chastity.

22. "Canticle of Brother Sun," slightly altered translation from Lawrence Cunningham, *Saint Francis of Assisi* (San Francisco: Harper & Row, 1981), 37-38, plus parts added by Francis in the same year, as cited in Julien Green, *God's Fool: The Life and Times of Francis of Assisi* (San Francisco: Harper & Row, 1985), 256-57, 259, 268. See ibid., 268-71 on "Sister Death" and the last hours of St. Francis.

Part IV

Finis

The secret of being boring is to tell all.
                              —F. M. A. de Voltaire

11

A Vision Begun

*The Devil is able to confront me with
arguments. Often he has offered an
argument of such weight that I didn't
know whether God exists or not.*
                              —Martin Luther

*The foolish and the dead alone never
change their opinion.*
                         —James Russell Lowell

I have barely scratched the surface of a vast subject.

What has created the fundamental comedy of this book—in some contrast to the other parts of my trilogy—is the concrete incongruity between death and life (with comedy as constituent to life). If the question of comedy is the question of how to live with incongruity, then, since death is the final incongruity, the ultimate question of comedy is the question of death. The present study thus embodies an integral contradiction, for it offers a more or less congruous exposition of an incongruous phenomenon.

Death is not part of life; death is the end of life. At the same time, the incommensurableness of comedy and death permits comedy to serve as a tiny weapon against death (just as death extinguishes comedy). Have we coveted any kind of peace between comedy and death? That would be to spoil everything—and it is out of the question anyway. Life and comedy can triumph only insofar as death is put to death. In a word, this book is a special kind of joke—as is the remainder of the trilogy. As Steve Martin has it, humor isn't pretty. I suggest that this last applies even more to the reaches of comedy, a category deeper and wider than humor as such.

The present volume closes with a summary-review of our subject, including a little criticism of my efforts together with some concluding observations and additional literary references. Twenty-one propositions follow, enumerated and classified in the interests of simplicity and organization. Certain of the more important contentions, presuppositions, and intimations of the overall study are iterated, usually in recouched form. The primary subjects of the propositions move, in obviously overlapping ways, from Comedy (1-7) to the Devil (8-14) to God (15-21). For the most part, this is a wrap-up.

Comedy

1. To be alive is to be caught up in comedy, for it is an all-pervasive presence. In this respect, the human "sense of humor" is as universal as the five bodily senses. However, just as one or more of the other senses may fail, so too the "sense of humor" can land itself in trouble. One sign that this sense is not functioning properly is the attempt, individual or collective, to reduce comedy to something that is only funny. Another sign that the comic sense is in trouble would consist in an automatic casting of aspersions upon things scatological. The campaign for scatology (not to be conducted in tacky fashion, I concede) is a blow against the Manichean impulse, a blow for the goodness of creation.

The grace of comedy may reduce, if by no more than a millimeter, the terrifying abyss between life and death.

2. What has been going on in this book, as in lesser measure through the other two volumes of my trilogy, is an elongated midrash upon Søren Kierkegaard, as embraced back in chapter one, "the more one suffers, the more has one a sense for the comic." (I should question the inverse of this; the comic seems to have *some* small redeeming quality.)

3. To try to grapple simultaneously with all three variables of Comedy/Devil/God is to become involved in issues of great analytical and practical complexity. Each variable alone is an enormous subject. Were, let us say, ten or twelve volumes to be allotted to the project—preferably with a team of writers—the task might be eased somewhat. With only three relatively brief volumes in hand, oversimplification remains a persisting problem.

I have found that we cannot keep apart gaiety and sobriety, sobriety and gaiety. For our acts of gaiety can only slightly soften the loud thanatopsic voices, while our acts of sobriety are punctured by a mischievous spontaneity, an *élan vital,* the Creation at work, God as Artist and Clown.

I am not sure that I have been able to establish adequately the relations between incongruity as such and funniness, particularly nonsense. Thus, if comedy (incongruity) is as serious a business as I have attempted to convey, how is it going to be linked to laughter? In this regard, I think that varying explanations of what makes people laugh remain unsatisfactory. We may never come to a convincing explanation. Laughter seems to be of "the nature of the beast." Perhaps the psychologist Norman N. Holland says the most that we can offer: "Why do we laugh? Because we are, as the children's song says, 'Free to be/You and me'"—the conclusion to his entire study of laughter.[1]

Comedy travels all over the place, mediating among freedom, justice, and propriety.

4. The dimension of comedy is vast but it is not identical with human existence as such. Beyond comedy stand at least two other dimensions of fundamental and equal significance for humankind: facticity (the brute way of things); and tragedy (catastrophe tied to necessity or fate). The first of these latter dimensions may be identified with Nature as such, which, while it may exhibit a comic aspect here and there, yet comprises overall a kind of neutral ground bursting only in potentiality. The second of the dimensions is well contrasted with comedy by Wylie Sypher: Tragic action, "however inspiring and however perfect in artistic form, runs through only one arc of the full cycle of drama; for the entire ceremonial cycle is birth: struggle: death: resurrection. The tragic arc is only birth: struggle: death. Consequently the range of comedy is wider than the tragic range—perhaps more fearless—and comic action can risk a different sort of purgation and triumph."[2]

Midrash: If we are raised from the dead, it will be quite in order to laugh; if we are not, Oblivion will have settled everything. In the latter case, Richard Dawkins will have been proved right: "The universe that we observe has precisely the properties we should expect if there is, at bottom, no design, no purpose, no evil and good, nothing but blind, pitiless indifference."[3] Yet, sadly for Dawkins, no one would/will be on hand to pay tribute to his finding.

5. Does it help or is it confusing to keep running back and forth from sober analysis to funniness? My reason for doing so is stated near the

start of chapter 6: the suddenness with which life transmogrifies tears into laughter, laughter into tears.

This may not satisfy you.

6. The trivializing of comedy is a serious affliction, a sign that a culture or society is not functioning all that well. Only "serious" things are then deemed "important." A collectivity that is unable to celebrate comedy as essential to life is sick, sick, sick. The other side of this point is the horrible metastasizing of "humor" into a place where people are commanded to do nothing other than laugh, as in the tyranny of a thousand TV laughtracks and their all pervading, degenerate assaults upon authentic comedy. Many true comedians—the Marx Brothers, Gracie Allen, Ernie Kovacs, *et alii*—must be turning in their graves.

7. In *Sitting in the Earth and Laughing,* Jewish humor is distinguished as the humor of a particular people. In contrast, as emphasized in *How To Tell God From the Devil,* Christian humor may be understood as involving a faith.[4] While the people/faith dichotomy is certainly valid in dealing with Jewishness/Christianness, I think I somewhat overdrew it in the context of comedy/humor. For in chapter 9 , any such difference is thrown into question by the presence of a comedy of *hutzpa k'lapei shamaya,* which certainly lives *inside* the ongoing faith of Judaism. (By implication, "comedy" is here pointed to as being deeper and broader than "humor.")

Devil

8. To deny the reality of the Devil (the personification of radical evil) is to fail to achieve a fulfilled and responsible theology and theological ethic—or, for that matter, a fulfilled humanity—since the Devil (granted a nondualist frame of reference) is the dark side of the God who is. Radical evil and suffering, and the terror of death, continue on. And we did not ask to exist. Overall, the world remains unredeemed. (This last is among the reasons why it is wrongheaded to claim that Christianity supersedes Judaism, although it is the ironic case that contemporary Judaism itself [not unlike the modern church] remains without a sufficiently forceful doctrine of the Devil—despite all the lessons ostensibly taught by the *Shoah.*)

Seen on the signboard of the Rockport, Massachusetts Baptist Church, 5 August 1993: "If you have a pain in the neck, thank God you're not a giraffe." Here in fourteen words are epitomized the almost studied irrelevance, even futility of much contemporary religiousness. For our pain may well be caused by cancer. The young wife of a colleague of mine was told—shortly before Christmas 1993—that she had cancer all through her body and would die very soon. There is a three-year-old son and a seven-year-old daughter. The young woman's prayer might well be, "Oh God, why do you have to behave like the Devil?" The Devil never weeps, cannot weep.

Jeffrey Burton Russell's concluding judgment in *The Devil* bears repeating: "The story of the Devil is grim, and any world view that ignores or denies the existential horror of evil is an illusion. Ivan's one child crying out alone in the darkness is worth the whole creation, *is* in a sense the creation. If any world view, theist or atheist, minimizes her suffering, declares it nonexistent, gives it elaborate philosophical justification, or explains it in terms of a greater good, whether the name assigned that good be God or the People, that world view renders her life, and yours, empty and vain."[5]

And yet: If the Devil is in fact the Shadow *of God,* is not unqualified irreverence toward the Devil describable as falling within the category of some kind of temptation *(Anfechtung)*?

9. The incongruity exuded by the dominion of death is itself made up dialectically of a mixture of incongruity and congruity. The incongruity arises from the fact that in death all the human unequals (rich and poor, powerful and powerless, male and female) are at once made equal. Yet, this latter development also creates congruity: a single status for all. Death effectuates a common peaceableness. Thus, presumably, the peaceful dead do not suffer from such horrors as clinical depression—unless there is some form of (traditionalist) hell.[6]

10. Human claims to possess absolute truth comprise an *imitatio diaboli*. But the human assertion of self-perfection is more woefully incongruous than such assertions on the part of Old Scratch himself. For the Devil is a manifestation of the divine. Thus, the lies of the Devil *(Druj)* are at least a (perverted) product of a divine heritage, whereas human lying is just lying.

11. The Devil is fought in three primary ways: theologically/ethically, politically, psychologically.

(a) The human laughter of scorn (sardonicism) directed against the Devil as Shadow of God is legitimated by the norm of righteousness as the

criterion of holiness (Isa. 5:16), a norm that has its source in God. When
Abraham asks, "Shall not the Judge of all the earth do what is just?" (Gen.
18:25), he is in fact saying that God ought to do what God Godself maintains to be just. Righteousness is hardly Abraham's invention.

God has to be encouraged, or perhaps even commanded, to persist in
the battle against the Devil, the divine Shadow. Jon D. Levenson shows
how by the time of the exile of the sixth century B.C.E., one major component (among many diverse components) of the spiritual life of Israel
was concern over Yahweh as a semiotiose deity, but one who can nevertheless be aroused to respond to anguished cries from the cultic community. This state of affairs helps to explain a great deal in the petitionary
prayer life of Israel, whereby God's inaction is lamented and demands
are forthcoming that God do better.

> Rouse yourself! Why do you
> sleep, O Lord?
> Awake, do not cast us off
> forever!
> Why do you hide your face?
> Why do you forget our
> affliction and oppression? (Ps. 44:23-24).

> How long, O God, is the foe to scoff?
> Is the enemy to revile your name forever?
> Why do you hold back your hand?
> why do you keep your hand in your bosom?...
> Rise up, O God, plead your cause;
> remember how the impious
> scoff at you all day long (Ps. 74:10-11, 22).

> Awake, awake, put on strength,
> O arm of the Lord! (Isa. 51:9).

As Levenson has earlier stated, "the failure of God is openly ac-
knowledged: no smug faith here, no flight into an otherworldly ideal.
But God is also *reproached* for his failure, told that it is neither inevi-
table nor excusable."[7]

David J. Wolpe comments that even God, in a certain midrashist's
"bold reading, cannot seek salvation alone. Thus Rabbi Abbahu's prayer,
quoting God's own declaration in the Psalms, claims that God needs
Rabbi Abbahu just as Rabbi Abbahu needs God: 'Lord of the universe,
You have said, "I am with him in distress." If You too suffer, save Your-

self. By heeding my prayers and pleas for redemption, bring about Your own salvation' (Tanh. B. Acharay 18). God must be prodded by the prayers of human beings to effect His own salvation!"[8]

Human prayers are—ought to be?—less for human salvation than they are—ought to be?—for the salvation of God.

(b) There must be unceasing and constantly renewing political action against "the wiles of the Devil…against the cosmic powers of this present darkness, against the spiritual forces of evil in the heavenly places" (Eph. 6:11-12). There must be a repairing and mending of a world (*tikkun olam*)[9] that has been broken by the Shadow as also by human sin, in imitation of and response to a politician God who is seeking—we trust—to make life more bearable but who ought to be doing a lot more.

Notoriously, of course, people often use God and religious beliefs in the interests of oppressing and exploiting others. In *The Politics of God* Kathryn Tanner argues that the Christian theological tradition can be freed from support for injustice and apolitical passivity and coupled to action for the sake of individual and social righteousness.[10] In *No Longer Aliens, No longer Strangers,* a study that relates Christian faith to Christian ethics, I seek to provide a theological foundation for social and political action: the moral life as essentially a matter of obedient response to the biblical God's justice and love in ways that emphasize unqualified human empowerment as the basic instrument for struggling against moral evil.[11]

Charlotte Perkins Gilman declares: "The Devil is a necessary component in male religion because a God without an adversary is inconceivable to the masculine mind."[12] The history of the oppression of females by males seems to vindicate Gilman's observation. But her finding points in an additional direction. To the extent that male mistreatment of females is overcome and women step up to equality, God is stepping out of the Shadow.

Applying Gilman's adversarial principle but *keeping ourselves from other considerations,* we may further comment that religious dualism will tend to show "masculinist" tendencies while religious monism will tend to show "feminist" ones. Further, the God/Devil dialectic that is put forward in the course of my trilogy will show a proclivity, or at least a wish, for masculinity/femininity together (in different wording, a converging of *animus/anima*).

Finally, and in awareness that to be the Devil is to make absolutist claims, emphasis should be placed upon the role of comedy and humor in fostering tolerance and social pluralism. Michael Mulkay writes of the power of humor to reproduce and allow for "the multiple realities of the social world. In this important respect, humor seems to be superior to ordinary, serious discourse, which is premised on an implicit denial of the fact that we live in a world of multiple meanings and multiple realities." In keeping with this distinction, Mulkay ends his sociological presentation of humor with the judgment that "perhaps the crucial task for those of us in search of truth is to create a way of communicating which will enable us [in Umberto Eco's words in *The Name of the Rose*] 'to make people laugh at truth, *to make truth laugh.*'"[13]

(c) We may affirm, or reaffirm, a great and proper need and place for a psychological, and particularly a psychoanalytic, orientation and perspective. In *How To Tell God From the Devil* I cite Jeffrey Burton Russell's judgment that the paradox of the Devil as manifestation of the divine yet, morally, a power to be fought "can be resolved in only one way: evil will be absorbed and controlled when it is integrated, and it will be integrated when it is fully recognized and understood. Not by *repression,* which only increases the shadow in the unconscious, but by conscious *suppression* of the evil elements that we have recognized in ourselves, will that element of the divine we call the Devil be brought out of chaos and out of opposition into order and under control."[14]

12. Death and the Devil are together shamed by a single reality: child-likeness. This it is that enables Kierkegaard to say two seemingly opposite but in fact complementary things: "the more one suffers, the more has one a sense for the comic," and comedy/humor recollects childhood.[15] The childlikeness of God is the death of the Devil.

13. The notion, "Though he kill me, yet I will trust in him" (Job 13:15),[16] is seen to verge upon moral incoherence in view of the fact that everyone is killed (or dies) sooner or later. *How can there be trust in the One who slays?*

14. The trial of God issues in an exile that begins to be ended, Christianly speaking, in the cross and the resurrection. In Jesus Christ, God shares flesh and blood "that through death he might destroy the one who has the power of death," the Devil (Heb. 2:14).

God

15. Is the life story of God a true one? That is to say, is the myth an authentic one?

Here is a life-and-death question. And I can supply no answer. The best I can do is to say that there may be an answer: In chapter 8 we include the words of Job 14:12a, "mortals lie down and do not rise again." Yet there is a "b": "until the heavens are no more, they will not awake, or be roused out of their sleep." An equation presents itself for our response: a + b = universal resurrection. Upon such a foundation as this, we may find ourselves at one with Emil Fackenheim: "The human astonishment, which is *terror* at a Presence at once divine and commanding," is empowered to turn "into a *second* astonishment, which is *joy*."[17]

What are the accompaniments and consequences of such an unproved and unprovable orientation as this?

16. The biblical God is, on the one hand, the fully free and sovereign power behind the universes and, on the other hand, a being "fragile in its loneliness and tormented by its need for our love."[18] "When God was alone in the universe [before creating human beings], He yearned for the company of His creations."[19]

God may not be so terribly unlike us after all, a consoling thought as perforce we face God in life and very shortly in death. The God that does battle with the Shadow is our Friend more than our Enemy. Indeed, God is our Friend precisely in that God is struggling, and will continue to struggle, against the Enemy.

17. Nevertheless: "The death question" continues on, calling the justice of God into question, an absolute question: How can "we love a God that is responsible for our death?" "The only way God can win the human heart is by freeing human beings from death. For only when the human heart is free from death are humans free to love God."[20]

We have been engaging ourselves in a practical, desperate exercise (an impossible dream?) in how to live with the evil-but-love/love-but-evil of the God who makes the universes and all that is therein. Some of the ways God has arranged and is arranging this world seem to us to be either stupid or perverse, or both. Just don't forget that you and I are fashioned in the image of God[21] and therefore we have not alone a capacity but also a right—within severe limits, of course—to distinguish what's stupid and perverse from what isn't stupid and perverse—a divinely implanted synderesis. To resort to terms from the world of medical insurance, the radical evil that human beings experience in life is more than divine incompetence; it may also be a matter of malpractice.[22] According to the Genesis story, human wickedness made God sorry that he had created humankind (6:5-6); a parallel from our side is that the divine wickedness—the pact with Satan—is enough to make us (who could never have sought to be born) sorry for having covenanted with God. Minimally speaking, it takes one klutz to know another klutz (from either side).

18. I suggest that beyond a natural human fear and reluctance to pass judgment upon God, one major cause of the unhappy and frequent inability to hold God finally culpable for radical evil and suffering—to put the blame where it in truth lies—is a failure in self-acceptance, that is, a failure of human beings to treat themselves as true possessors of the divine image. A full realization of the *imago dei* as a fact entails *unreserved* moral judgment, the sort of thing in which God Godself engages. Put morally/theologically, one or another human refusal to judge God is a form of unfaithfulness to God, a failure in the obligation taught to us by God. Paradoxically, it betrays the very will of God, the God who is entirely prepared and entirely willing (in God's free grace) to be judged, to be accountable, to be obligated.

This graceful readiness of God, on the one hand, prevents comedy and humor about God from being blasphemous, and, on the other hand, makes possible the divine comedy. In an epigraph to the third part of this book Elie Wiesel speaks not just of laughter but of metaphysical laughter—as a way to avoid the diminishing of God.[23]

19. If the divine acceptance of the human is incongruous, so too the only morally acceptable response of God to human charges of blameworthiness and sin is the comedy (incongruity) of penitential, saving acts.

20. To be accepted by the God beyond the gods is an incongruity, due to the hiatus between the human and the divine, but the *shalom* that ensues lives beyond incongruity, pointing as it does to a final congruity that is redemption, a Comedy beyond comedy.

A Cistercian tale is told of an *idiota* (illiterate rustic) about to die of cancer. Upon his death bed, having been given something to drink, this idiot, who had never learned to sing or read, broke into "certain new and utterly delightful hymns and canticles from the Songs of Sion. He was insulting death, as though saying to death, Where is your victory?"

"Here am I, a great sinner and poor little beggar man. Since I have borne patiently the marks of the Lord Jesus in my body for his name's sake, I do not fear you, ghostly shade, mother of sorrow, exterminator of joy and waster of life. No, I despise you, because I know you have been swallowed up and utterly destroyed in the victory of the cross of my Lord Jesus Christ." So this precentor of ours, chanting Alleluia, that song of the streets of the heavenly Jerusalem, as it were anticipating it, revealed in wonderful prophecy what would happen to him after the death of the flesh, while still lodged in the corruptible flesh. Thus rejoicing and praising with a voice of exultation and testimony he gave up his blessed spirit.[24]

Most unbearable/most impossible/most comedic/most assuring midrash: *In order to despise death, our idiot must despise the Devil, father of Death, and thus is he called to despise the Shadow, the dark side of God. But the dark side of God is still God. Therefore, the only victory over Death that there can be is God's victory over Godself, wherein we are empowered to cease despising God as Enemy and to embrace God as Friend.*

Down in the late twentieth century, a ten-year-old girl named Leah could not know that she was to be little sister to our Cistercian *idiota,* despite a gap of hundreds of years. For Leah developed acute leukemia, of a kind poorly responsive to chemotherapy. Robert Coles the child psychiatrist tells of his meeting with a group of five children in Brookline, Massachusetts after the diagnosis of Leah's condition had been made: "It was then that I heard God questioned as I never had before by children explicitly 'religious' in their background, education, stated beliefs. 'How can God let such a thing happen?' 'Why—why does He permit this?' '*What*, tell me, what has she done to deserve this?' 'Where is He, where is God?'..."[25]

Commenting that while in *The Hidden God* Samuel Balentine is of course correct to translate the Hebrew *lamah* by the interrogative "why," G. Tom Milazzo maintains that Balentine nevertheless

seems to miss much of the force of the use of the interrogative in Hebrew Scripture. To ask *lamah* of God is indeed to ask why God has chosen to remain silent. More is at stake, however. To ask why God is silent is to place the issue of human suffering before and in front of God. To ask God why humans suffer and die is to ask for what reason, for what purpose, to what end, God has chosen to hide itself in darkness. Thus, to ask God why it has chosen to hide itself is also to ask what reason or purpose hiddenness fulfills, or even to what end God has chosen hiddenness. To ask God to disclose the reason God has hidden itself is to ask God to put human suffering into perspective by providing access to the reason for God's hiddenness. In effect, the experience of human suffering becomes tied to the issue of divine responsibility.[26]

It was precisely in the above way that the five children of Brookline, Massachusetts were asking "Why?"

Dr. Coles then closes the story of Leah:

> I remember my last visit to Leah. She was not far from death. Her body had withered; she was jaundiced, dehydrated, sweaty, feverish. At her bedside was her father's Bible. Nearby, her mother sewed and sang a song the girl's grandmother (now dead) had loved, had taught Leah years earlier: "Three o'clock in the morning; we danced the whole night through." It was a romantic ballad from the 1920s and somehow meant a lot to Leah, for whom it was a pitch-black, melancholy three o'clock, with only a handful of sunrises left. Her eyes shone, however, and she listened carefully, her mind and soul bravely alert. I saw in Leah a child intensely attached to a family's religious and spiritual life, its prayers and food and ceremonies, its spoken acknowledgment of the Lord, its remembrance of His words, of what He and His people had experienced together in the past and were still, in that hospital room, in our time, undergoing together. "I'd like to go to that 'high rock,'" Leah told her dad just before she slipped into a final coma—and from then until her death, her heartbroken but proud and strong father could be heard by nurses and doctors and ward helpers and visitors and family members saying in Hebrew the 61st Psalm: "Hear my cry, O God; attend unto my prayer. From the end of the earth will I cry unto thee, when my heart is overwhelmed: lead me to the rock that is higher than I." The rock for Leah, for her family, was a Judaism that would not break or yield, even at the death of a young girl.[27]

21. From all our anger with God we are led into God's comedy. From there we are brought to the love of God, of the neighbor, and of the stranger. And thence do we pass to the *shalom* that outdistances death.

The suffering of God "cannot be a full answer to the problem of suffering. To suffer with someone is better than to suffer alone, but it is better still to be spared."[28] Death remains as abandonment, as forgottenness,[29] and human beings have no power to put death to death. Therefore, the One who laughs at death must come—to dissolve abandonment, to remember all that has been forgotten, to destroy death itself.

The Queen/King of the Universe is forbidden to laugh until the divine weeping is done, until all human weeping is done. For while the source of comedy is weeping, the end of weeping is prayer. Comedy and prayer become as one. The solitary prayer of God, "may it be my will that my mercy overcome my anger," gains its counterpart in the solitary (*einzeln*) prayer of humankind, as given voice by a young man called Benjamin of the village of Zemyock. Benjamin has just reached the terrifying conclusion that were God not to be, Zemyock would become no more than an absurd fragment of the universe. And so he prays: "If you do not exist, where does all the suffering go? It goes for nothing. Oh, my God, it goes for nothing!"[30]

Notes

1. Norman N. Holland, *Laughing: A Psychology of Humor* (Ithaca-London: Cornell University Press, 1982), 199.
2. Wylie Sypher, as cited without a source reference in Holland, *Laughing,* 97. Consult also Wendy Farley, *Tragic Vision and Divine Compassion: A Contemporary Theodicy* (Louisville: Westminster/John Knox Press, 1990); and E. J. Tinsley, *Christian Theology and the Frontiers of Tragedy* (Leeds: Leeds University Press, 1963).
3. Richard Dawkins, "The Method in This Madness, *The Sunday Times* (London), 9 January 1994, "The Culture," 14-15.
4. A. Roy Eckardt, *Sitting in the Earth and Laughing* (New Brunswick and London: Transaction Publishers, Rutgers University, 1992), chap. 11; *How To Tell God From the Devil* (New Brunswick and London: Transaction Publishers, Rutgers University, 1995) (hereinafter HTT), chap. 8. Cf. Steve Lipman, "Jewish Humor," chap. 5 of *Laughter In Hell: The Use of Humor During the Holocaust* (Northvale, N.J. and London: Jason Aronson, 1991); and *Humor* 4-2 (1991): special number on Jewish humor.
5. Jeffrey Burton Russell, *The Devil: Perceptions of Evil from Antiquity to Primitive Christianity* (Ithaca and London: Cornell University Press, 1987), 260.
6. Cf. Alan E. Bernstein, *The Formation of Hell: Death and Retribution in the Ancient and Early Christian Worlds* (Ithaca and London: Cornell University Press, 1993).
7. Jon D. Levenson, *Creation and the Persistence of Evil* (San Francisco: Harper & Row, 1988), 50, 24. I provide a fuller exposition of Levenson's work in HTT, chap. 3.
8. David J. Wolpe, *The Healer of Shattered Hearts* (New York: Henry Holt, 1990), 13.
9. Emil L. Fackenheim, *To Mend the World: Foundations of Future Jewish Thought* (New York: Schocken Books, 1982). On "the powers" as good and evil, see Letty M. Russell, *Household of Freedom: Authority in Feminist Theology* (Philadelphia: Westminster Press, 1987), 77-82; more intensively, Walter Wink, *Naming the Powers* (Philadelphia: Fortress Press, 1984); *Unmasking the Powers* (Philadelphia: Fortress Press, 1986); *Engaging the Powers* (Minneapolis: Fortress Press, 1992).
10. Kathryn Tanner, *The Politics of God: Christian Theologies and Social Justice* (Minneapolis: Fortress Press, 1992). Tanner singles out beliefs in God's transcendence and what she calls God's "universal providential agency" (31, 98-107). See also Sharon D. Welch, *A Feminist Ethic of Risk* (Minneapolis: Fortress Press, 1990), and Glenn Tinder, *The Political Meaning of Christianity* (Baton Rouge and London: Louisiana State University Press, 1989).
11. A. Roy Eckardt, *No Longer Aliens, No Longer Strangers: Christian Faith and Ethics for Today* (Atlanta: Scholars Press, 1994), chaps. 6, 7. Consult also my full-length study in Christian theological ethics, *For Righteousness' Sake: Contemporary Moral Philosophies* (Bloomington: Indiana University Press, 1987).
12. Charlotte Perkins Gilman, as cited in Gloria Kaufman, ed., *In Stitches: A Patchwork of Feminist Humor and Satire* (Bloomington: Indiana University Press, 1991), 171.
13. Michael Mulkay, *On Humor: Its Nature and Its Place in Modern Society* (Cambridge: Basil Blackwell, 1988), 219, 223. Scientific discourse, although it be-

longs to a fully serious mode, is not as absolutist as other forms of discourse. For a (post-Christian) theological exposition that opposes the absolutizing of Christian faith, together with a denial that Jesus Christ is related to God in a way qualitatively different from other human beings, consult Daphne Hampson, *Theology and Feminism* (Oxford: Basil Blackwell, 1990).

14. Russell, *The Devil*, 32; cited in HTT, chap. 1. Consult also Ernest Becker's social-psychological study, *Escape From Evil* (New York: Free Press, 1975).

15. The second assertion is reported in Holland, *Laughing*, 100.

16. The verse is translated in the NRSV as "See, he will kill me; I have no hope."

17. Emil Fackenheim, *God's Presence in History: Jewish Affirmations and Philosophical Reflections* (New York: New York University Press, 1970), 16.

18. G. Thomas Milazzo, *The Protest and the Silence: Suffering, Death, and Biblical Theology* (Minneapolis: Augsburg Fortress Press, 1991), 48. In re: Milazzo's use of "it" for God, he may be trying to avoid sexist language. In a separate analysis, Milazzo indicates that his employment of the third person neuter in language about God is also a device for avoiding anthropomorphism ("To An Impotent God: Images of Divine Impotence in Hebrew Scripture," *Shofar* 11, 2 [1993]: 30n). "This impotent god walked the road to Babylon and stood among the crematoria at Auschwitz" (ibid., 49).

19. *Numbers Rabbah* 13:6, as quoted in Wolpe, *Healer of Shattered Hearts*, 14. Consult "The Divine Pathos," *Between God and Man: An Interpretation of Judaism, From the Writings of Abraham Joshua Heschel*, ed. Fritz A. Rothschild (New York: Free Press, 1959); more generally, Abraham Joshua Heschel, *The Prophets*, 2 vols. (New York: Harper & Row, 1962).

20. Milazzo, *The Protest and the Silence*, 161, 159. See, in this connection, John Hick, "Present and Future Life," in *A John Hick Reader*, ed. Paul Badham (London: Macmillan, 1990), 145—60.

21. The *imago dei* is what makes possible the affirmation that "when one person greets another it is as if he greets the Divine presence" (*Mechilta, Amalek*, as cited in Wolpe, *Healer of Shattered Hearts*, 113).

22. *The Oxford Universal Dictionary* defines "act of God" as "the action of uncontrollable natural forces in causing an accident." Here is linguistic secularization captured by absurdity.

23. Elie Wiesel, *Souls on Fire* (New York: Vintage Books, 1973), 198-99.

24. Conrad of Eberbach, *Exordium magnum Cisterciense*, ed. B. Griesser (Rome, 1961), iv, 16, 242, as cited in John Saward, *Perfect Fools* (Oxford: Oxford University Press, 1980), 65—66.

25. Robert Coles, *The Spiritual Life of Children* (Boston: Houghton Mifflin, 1990), 274.

26. Milazzo, *The Protest and the Silence*, 43.

27. Coles, *Spiritual Life of Children*, 276. In other chapters Coles recounts the spiritual life of non-Jewish children: Christian, Islamic, secular (chaps. 9, 10, 12), and ends with "The Child as Pilgrim" (chap. 13).

28. Wolpe, *Healer of Shattered Hearts*, 149.

29. Milazzo, *The Protest and the Silence*, 41-42.

30. André Schwarz-Bart, *The Last of the Just*, trans. Stephen Becker (New York: Atheneum, 1961), 69.

Bibliography

Aichele, George, Jr. *Theology as Comedy: Critical and Theoretical Implications*. Lanham, Md.: University Press of America, 1980.

Allen, Woody. *Without Feathers-Getting Even-Side Effects*. New York: Quality Paperback Book Club, 1989.

Anderson, Bernhard W. *Creation versus Chaos: The Reinterpretation of Mythical Symbolism in the Bible*. Philadelphia: Fortress Press, 1987.

Apte, Mahadev L. *Humor and Laughter: An Anthropological Approach*. Ithaca and London: Cornell University Press, 1985.

Armstrong, Karen. *A History of God*. New York: Alfred A. Knopf, 1993.

Arnold, Patrick M. *Wildmen, Warriors, and Kings: Masculine Spirituality and the Bible*. New York: Crossroad, 1991.

Bailey, Lloyd R., Sr. *Biblical Perspectives on Death*. Philadelphia: Fortress Press, 1979.

Becker, Ernest. *The Denial of Death*. New York: Free Press, 1973.

_____. *Escape From Evil*. New York: Free Press, 1975.

Beker, J. Christiaan. *Suffering and Hope*, rev. ed. Grand Rapids: Wm. B. Eerdmans, 1994.

Bernstein, Alan E. *The Formation of Hell: Death and Retribution in the Ancient and Early Christian Worlds*. Ithaca and London: Cornell University Press, 1993.

Birch, Charles, William Eakin, and Jay B. McDaniel, eds. *Liberating Life: Contemporary Approaches to Ecological Theology*. Maryknoll: Orbis Books, 1990.

Brandon, S. G. F. *The Judgment of the Dead: The Idea of Life After Death in the Major Religions*. New York: Charles Scribner's Sons, 1967.

Brodkey, Harold. "Dying: An Update." *The New Yorker* (7 February 1994): 70 ff.

Bulkeley, Kelly. *The Wilderness of Dreams: Exploring the Religious Meanings of Dreams in Modern Western Culture*. Albany: State University of New York Press, 1993.

Callahan, Daniel. *The Troubled Dream of Life: Living With Mortality*. New York: Simon & Schuster, 1993.

Camus, Albert. *The Fall*, trans. Justin O'Brien. New York: Vintage Books, 1956.

_____. *The Rebel.* New York: Vintage, 1956.

_____. "The Renegade." In *Exile and the Kingdom,* trans. Justin O'Brien. New York: Alfred A. Knopf, 1958.

_____. *The Stranger,* trans. Stuart Gilbert. New York: Vintage Books, 1946.

Carr, Anne E. *Transforming Grace: Christian Tradition and Women's Experience.* San Francisco: Harper & Row, 1988.

Cobb, John B., Jr. *Matters of Life and Death.* Louisville: Westminster/John Knox Press, 1991.

Cobb, John B., Jr., and Christopher Ives, eds. *The Emptying God: A Buddhist-Jewish-Christian Conversation.* Maryknoll, N.Y.: Orbis Books, 1990.

Cohen, Arthur. *The Tremendum: A Theological Interpretation of the Holocaust.* New York: Crossroad, 1981.

Cohen, Leonard. *Stranger Music: Selected Poems and Songs.* New York: Pantheon Books, 1993.

Coles, Robert. *The Call of Service: A Witness to Idealism.* Boston: Houghton Mifflin, 1993.

_____. *The Spiritual Life of Children.* Boston: Houghton Mifflin, 1990.

Continuum 2, 2-3 (1993). Special issue on "Ideas of the Holy."

Culbertson, Philip. *New Adam: The Future of Male Spirituality.* Minneapolis: Fortress Press, 1992.

Davies, Christie. *Ethnic Humor Around the World: A Comparative Analysis.* Bloomington: Indiana University Press, 1990.

Davis, Stephen T., ed. *Encountering Evil: Live Options in Theodicy.* Atlanta: John Knox Press, 1981.

Delaney, Gayle, ed. *New Directions in Dream Interpretation.* Albany: State University of New York Press, 1993.

Donnelly, Doris. "Divine Folly: Being Religious and the Exercise of Humor." *Theology Today* 48 (1992): 385-98.

The Door (bi-monthly).

Driver, Tom. *Christ in a Changing World: Toward an Ethical Christology.* New York: Crossroad, 1981.

Durant, J., and C. J. Miller, eds. *Laughing Matters: A Serious Look at Humor.* New York: John Wiley, 1988.

Eckardt, A. Roy. "Between the Angelic and the Diabolic: A Postmodern Interpretation." *Theology Today* 52 (1994): 1-11.

_____. *Black-Woman-Jew: Three Wars for Human Liberation.* Bloomington: Indiana University Press, 1989.

_____. *Collecting Myself: A Writer's Retrospective,* ed. Alice L. Eckardt. Atlanta: Scholars Press, 1993.

_____. "Death in the Judaic and Christian Traditions," in Arien Mack, ed., *Death in American Experience.* New York: Schocken Books, 1973, 123-48.

_____. "Divine Incongruity: Comedy and Tragedy in a Post-Holocaust World." *Theology Today* 48 (1992): 399–412.

_____. *For Righteousness' Sake: Contemporary Moral Philosophies.* Bloomington: Indiana University Press, 1987.

_____. *How To Tell God From the Devil: On the Way to Comedy.* New Brunswick and London: Transaction Publishers, Rutgers University, 1995.

_____. *No Longer Aliens, No Longer Strangers: Christian Faith and Ethics for Today.* Atlanta: Scholars Press, 1994.

_____. *Reclaiming the Jesus of History: Christology Today.* Minneapolis: Fortress Press, 1992.

_____. *Sitting in the Earth and Laughing: A Handbook of Humor.* New Brunswick and London: Transaction Publishers, Rutgers University, 1992.

_____. "The Ugliest Customer: A Life History of Death." *Encounter* 55 (1994): 51–59.

Eckardt, Alice L., and A. Roy Eckardt. *Long Night's Journey Into Day: A Revised Retrospective on the Holocaust.* Detroit: Wayne State University Press; Oxford: Pergamon Press, 1988.

Eilbert, Henry. *What Is A Jewish Joke? An Excursion into Jewish Humor.* Northvale, N.J. and London: Jason Aronson, 1993.

Elias, Norbert. *The Loneliness of the Dying,* trans. Edmund Jephcott. Oxford: Basil Blackwell, 1985.

Excerpts From the Diaries Of the Late God, ed. Anthony Towne. New York: Harper & Row, 1968.

Fackenheim, Emil. *The Jewish Thought of Emil Fackenheim: A Reader,* ed. Michael L. Morgan. Detroit: Wayne State University Press, 1987.

_____. *To Mend the World: Foundations of Future Jewish Thought.* New York: Schocken Books, 1982.

_____. *What Is Judaism? An Interpretation for the Present Age.* New York: Summit Books, 1987.

Farley, Wendy. *Tragic Vision and Divine Compassion: A Contemporary Theodicy.* Louisville: Westminster/John Knox Press, 1990.

Fasching, Darrell J. *The Ethical Challenge of Auschwitz and Hiroshima: Apocalypse or Utopia?* Albany: State University of New York Press, 1993.

_____. *Narrative Theology After Auschwitz: From Alienation to Ethics.* Minneapolis: Fortress Press, 1992.

Fischer, John M., ed. *The Metaphysics of Death.* Stanford: Stanford University Press, 1993.

Frankel, Ellen. *The Classic Tales: 4,000 Years of Jewish Lore.* Northvale, N.J. and London: Jason Aronson, 1993.

Freud, Sigmund. *Jokes and Their Relation to the Unconscious,* trans. James Strachey. New York: Norton, 1960.

Frieden, Betty. *The Fountain of Age*. New York: Simon & Schuster, 1993.

Galligan, Edward L. *The Comic Vision in Literature*. Athens: University of Georgia Press, 1984.

Girardot, Norman J. *Myth and Meaning in Early Taoism: The Theme of Chaos (hun-tun)*. Berkeley and London: University of California Press, 1983.

God: The Ultimate Autobiography. London: Pan Books, 1989.

González-Crussi, F. "Days of the Dead." *The New Yorker* (1 November 1993): 71 ff.

Gopnik, Adam. "Steve Martin: The Late Period." *The New Yorker* (29 November 1993): 98–113.

Green, Julien. *God's Fool: The Life and Times of Francis of Assisi*. San Francisco: Harper & Row, 1985.

Greenberg, Irving. *The Jewish Way: Living the Holidays*. New York: Summit Books, 1988.

Gritsch, Eric. *Martin—God's Court Jester: Luther in Retrospect*. Philadelphia: Fortress Press, 1983.

Gutwirth, Marcel. *Laughing Matter: An Essay on the Comic*. Ithaca and London: Cornell University Press, 1993.

Haig, Robin Andrew. *The Anatomy of Humor: Biopsychological and Therapeutic Perspectives*. Springfield, Ill.: Charles Thomas, 1988.

Hampson, Daphne. *Theology and Feminism*. Oxford: Basil Blackwell, 1990.

Hawking, Stephen. *Black Holes and Baby Universes*. New York: Bantam Books, 1993.

Haynes, Stephen R. *Prospects for Post-Holocaust Theology*. Atlanta: Scholars Press, 1991.

Heschel, Abraham Joshua. *Between God and Man: An Interpretation of Judaism,* selected and ed. by Fritz A. Rothschild. New York: Free Press, 1959.

_____. *The Prophets*, 2 vols. New York: Harper & Row, 1962.

Heyward, Isabel Carter. *The Redemption of God: A Theology of Mutual Relation*. Washington: University Press of America, 1982.

Hick, John. *Death and Eternal Life*. Louisville: Westminster/John Knox Press, 1994.

_____. *A John Hick Reader,* ed. Paul Badham. London: Macmillan, 1990.

Holland, Norman N. *Laughing: A Psychology of Humor*. Ithaca and London: Cornell University Press, 1982.

Humor: International Journal of Humor Research (quarterly).

Hyers, Conrad. *And God Created Laughter: The Bible as Divine Comedy*. Atlanta: John Knox Press, 1987.

_____. *The Comic Vision and the Christian Faith: A Celebration of Life and Laughter*. New York: Pilgrim Press, 1981.

_____, ed. *Holy Laughter: Essays on Religion in the Comic Perspective*. New York: Seabury Press, 1969.

Irwin, Robert. *The Arabian Nightmare* (a novel). New York: Viking Penguin, 1987.

Jiménez, Juan Ramón. *Platero y Yo: Elegía Andaluza, 1907–1916.* Buenos Aires: Editorial Losada, S.A., 1942.

Johnson, Elizabeth A. *Consider Jesus: Waves of Renewal in Christology.* London: Geoffrey Chapman, 1990.

_____. *She Who Is: The Mystery of God in Feminist Theological Literature.* New York: Crossroad, 1993.

Judy, Dwight H. *Healing the Male Soul: Christianity and the Mythic Journey.* New York: Crossroad, 1992.

Jung, C. G. *Aion: Researches Into the Phenomenology of the Self. Collected Works* 9, II, trans. R. F. C. Hull. London: Routledge & Kegan Paul, 1959.

_____. *The Archetypes and the Collective Unconscious. Collected Works* 9, I, trans. R. F. C. Hull. London: Routledge & Kegan Paul, 1959.

_____. *Civilization in Transition. Collected Works* 10, trans. R. F. C. Hull. London: Routledge & Kegan Paul, 1964.

Kafka, Franz. *The Trial,* trans. Willa and Edwin Muir. New York: Schocken Books, 1968.

Kaufman, Gloria, ed. *In Stitches: A Patchwork of Feminist Humor and Satire.* Bloomington: Indiana University Press, 1991.

Kaufman, Gordon D. *In Face of Mystery: A Constructive Theology.* Cambridge: Harvard University Press, 1993.

Kazin, Alfred. "Jews: Personal History." *The New Yorker* (7 March 1994): 62 ff.

Kierkegaard, Søren. *Parables of Kierkegaard,* ed. Thomas C. Oden. Princeton: Princeton University Press, 1978.

Koestler, Arthur. *The Act of Creation.* New York: Dell Publishing Co., 1967.

Kuralt, Charles. *A Life on the Road.* New York: G. P. Putnam's Sons, 1990.

Lang, Candace. *Irony/Humor: Critical Paradigms.* Baltimore: Johns Hopkins University Press, 1988.

Laytner, Anson. *Arguing With God: A Jewish Tradition.* Northvale, N.J. and London: Jason Aronson, 1990.

Lear, Edward. *The Nonsense Books of Edward Lear.* New York: New American Library, 1961.

Levenson, Jon D. *Creation and the Persistence of Evil: The Jewish Drama of Divine Omnipotence.* San Francisco: Harper & Row, 1988.

Levin, Harry. *Playboys and Killjoys: An Essay on the Theory and Practice of Comedy.* New York: Oxford University Press, 1987.

L'Heureux, John. *Comedians.* New York: Viking Penguin, 1990.

Linzey, Andrew. *Christianity and the Rights of Animals.* New York: Crossroad, 1987.

Lipman, Steve. *Laughter in Hell: The Use of Humor during the Holocaust.* Northvale, N.J. and London: Jason Aronson, 1991.

McCann, Graham. *Woody Allen: New Yorker*. Cambridge: Polity Press, 1990.

Maccoby, Hyam, compiler and translator. *The Day God Laughed: Sayings, Fables and Entertainments of the Jewish Sages*. New York: St. Martin's Press, 1978.

McFague, Sallie. *The Body of God: An Ecological Theology*. Minneapolis: Fortress Press, 1993.

_____. *Models of God: Theology for an Ecological, Nuclear Age*. Philadelphia: Fortress Press, 1987.

MacGregor, Geddes. *Angels: Ministers of Grace*. New York: Paragon House, 1988.

Maclean, Dorothy. *To Hear the Angels Sing*. Middleton, Wis.: Lorian Press, 1980.

McTavish, John. "John Updike and the Funny Theologian." *Theology Today* 48 (1992): 413–25.

Martin, Malachi. *Hostage to the Devil: The Possession and Exorcism of Five Living Americans*. San Francisco: HarperSanFrancisco, 1992.

Maurois, André. *Illusions*. New York: Columbia University Press, 1968.

May, Rollo. *The Cry For Myth*. New York: W. W. Norton, 1991.

Mehta, Ved. *Fly and the Fly-Bottle: Encounters with British Intellectuals*. New York: Columbia University Press, 1983.

Metz, Johann Baptist. *Faith in History and Society: Toward a Practical Fundamental Theology*, trans. David Smith. New York: Seabury Press, 1980.

Meyers, Diana T. *Self, Society, and Personal Choice*. New York: Columbia University Press, 1989.

Milazzo, G. Tom. *The Protest and the Silence: Suffering, Death, and Biblical Theology*. Minneapolis: Augsburg Fortress Press, 1991.

_____. "To An Impotent God: Images of Divine Impotence in Hebrew Scripture." *Shofar* 11 (Winter 1993): 30–49.

Moffitt, Alan, Milton Kramer, and Robert Hoffmann, eds. *The Functions of Dreaming*. Albany: State University of New York Press, 1993.

Morreall, John, ed. *The Philosophy of Laughter and Humor*. Albany: State University of New York Press, 1987.

_____. *Taking Laughter Seriously*. Albany: State University of New York Press, 1983.

Murray, Henry A. *Endeavors in Psychology: Selections from the Personology of Henry A. Murray*, ed. Edwin S. Shneidman. New York: Harper & Row, 1981.

Nelson, James B. *Body Theology*. Louisville: Westminster/John Knox Press, 1992.

Niebuhr, Reinhold. *The Self and the Dramas of History*. New York: Charles Scribner's Sons, 1955.

Niebuhr, Richard R. *Resurrection and Historical Reason: A Study of Theological Method.* New York: Charles Scribner's Sons, 1957.

Novak, William, and Moshe Waldoks. *The Big Book of Jewish Humor.* New York: Harper & Row, 1981.

Nozick, Robert. *The Nature of Rationality.* Princeton: Princeton University Press, 1993.

Nuland, Sherwin B. *How We Die.* New York: Alfred A. Knopf, 1994.

O'Brien, Edna. *House of Splendid Isolation* (a novel). London: Weidenfeld & Nicolson, 1994.

Oliver, Harold H. "The Neglect and Recovery of Nature in Twentieth-Century Protestant Thought." *Journal of the American Academy of Religion* 60 (1992): 379–404.

Olsen, Lance. *Circus of the Mind in Motion: Postmodernism and the Comic Vision.* Detroit: Wayne State University Press, 1990.

Oring, Elliott. *Jokes and Their Relations.* Lexington: University Press of Kentucky, 1992.

Paulos, John Allen. *Mathematics and Humor.* Chicago and London: University of Chicago Press, 1982.

Pinchas, Charles, and Jay B. McDaniel, eds. *Good News for Animals? Christian Approaches to Animal Well-Being.* Maryknoll, N.Y.: Orbis Books, 1993.

Religious Education 85 (1990), special number on "The Pedagogy of Death."

Religious Education 84 (1989), special number on "Theodicy and Religious Education."

Russell, Jeffrey Burton. *The Devil: Perceptions of Evil from Antiquity to Primitive Christianity.* Ithaca and London: Cornell University Press, 1987.

_____. *Lucifer: The Devil in the Middle Ages.* Ithaca and London: Cornell University Press, 1986.

_____. *Mephistopheles: The Devil in the Modern World.* Ithaca and London: Cornell University Press, 1990.

_____. *The Prince of Darkness: Radical Evil and the Power of Good in History.* Ithaca and London: Cornell University Press, 1992.

_____. *Satan: The Early Christian Tradition.* Ithaca and London: Cornell University Press, 1987.

Russell, Letty M. *Household of Freedom: Authority in Feminist Theology.* Philadelphia: Westminster Press, 1987.

Russell, Roy. *Life, Mind, and Laughter.* Chicago: Adams, 1987.

Sands, Kathleen M. *Evil and Tragedy in Feminist Theology.* Minneapolis: Fortress Press, 1994.

Sartre, Jean-Paul. *The Devil & the Good Lord*, a play in three acts, trans. Kitty Black. New York: Alfred A. Knopf, 1960.

Satan: The Hiss and Tell Memoirs. London: Pan Books, 1989.

Savater, Fernando. *Childhood Regained: The Art of the Storyteller,* trans. Frances M. López-Morillas. New York: Columbia University Press, 1982.

Saward, John. *Perfect Fools: Folly for Christ's Sake in Catholic and Orthodox Spirituality.* Oxford: Oxford University Press, 1980.

Schulz, Charles M. *And the Beagles and the Bunnies Shall Lie Down Together: The Theology in Peanuts.* Horsham, West Sussex: Ravette Books, 1990.

Schwartz, Howard, compiler and ed. *Gabriel's Palace: Jewish Mystical Tales.* New York-Oxford: Oxford University Press, 1993.

Shalit, Gene, ed. *Laughing Matters: A Celebration of American Humor.* New York: Barnes & Noble, 1993.

Singer, June. *Boundaries of the Soul.* Garden City, N.Y.: Doubleday Anchor Books, 1977.

Smith, Mark S. *The Early History of God: Yahweh and the Other Deities in Ancient Israel.* San Francisco: Harper & Row, 1990.

Swabey, Marie Collins. *Comic Laughter: A Philosophical Essay.* Hamden, Conn.: Archon Books, 1970.

Tanner, Kathryn. *The Politics of God: Christian Theologies and Social Justice.* Minneapolis: Fortress Press, 1992.

"Tears and Laughter: The Joan and Melissa Rivers Story." NBC Television, 15 May 1994.

Telushkin, Joseph. *Jewish Humor: What the Best Jewish Jokes Say About the Jews.* New York: William Morrow, 1992.

Tillich, Paul. *The Courage To Be.* New Haven: Yale University Press, 1952.

Tinder, Glenn. *The Political Meaning of Christianity: An Interpretation.* Baton Rouge and London: Louisiana State University Press, 1989.

Tinsley, E. J. *Christian Theology and the Frontiers of Tragedy.* Leeds: Leeds University Press, 1963.

Townes, Emilie M., ed. *A Troubling in My Soul: Womenist Perspectives on Evil and Suffering.* Maryknoll, N.Y.: Orbis Books, 1994.

Trout, Kilgore (pseud.). *Venus on the Half-Shell.* New York: Dell Pub. Co., 1980.

Vermes, Pamela. *The Riddle of the Sparks.* Oxford: Foxcombe Press, 1993.

Walker, Nancy A. *A Very Serious Thing: Women's Humor and American Culture.* Minneapolis: University of Minnesota Press, 1988.

Wallace, Mark I. "The Wild Bird Who Heals: Recovering the Spirit in Nature." *Theology Today* 50 (1993): 13-28.

Welch, Sharon D. *A Feminist Ethic of Risk.* Minneapolis: Fortress Press, 1990.

White, E. B. *The Second Tree from the Corner.* New York: Harper & Row, 1989.

Wiesel, Elie. *"Ani Maamin":* A Song Lost and Found Again, trans. Marion Wiesel. New York: Random House, 1973.

_____. *The Forgotten*, trans. Stephen Becker. New York: Summit Books, 1992.

_____. *The Gates of the Forest*, trans. Frances Frenaye. New York: Avon Books, 1967.

_____. *Somewhere a Master: Further Hasidic Portraits and Legends*, trans. Marion Wiesel. New York: Summit Books, 1982.

_____. *Souls on Fire: Portraits and Legends of Hasidic Masters*. New York: Vintage Books, 1973.

_____. *The Trial of God (as it was held on February 25, 1649, in Shamgorod)*, a play in three acts, trans. Marion Wiesel. New York: Random House, 1979.

Willimon, William H., compiler. *And the Laugh Shall Be First: A Treasury of Religious Humor*. Nashville: Abingdon Press, 1986.

_____, compiler. *Last Laugh*. Nashville: Abingdon Press, 1991.

Wink, Walter. *Engaging the Powers: Discernment and Resistance in a World of Domination*. Minneapolis: Fortress Press, 1992.

_____. *Naming the Powers: The Language of Power in the New Testament*. Philadelphia: Fortress Press, 1984.

_____. *Unmasking the Powers: The Invisible Powers That Determine Human Existence*. Philadelphia: Fortress Press, 1986.

Wolff, Pierre. *May I Hate God?* New York: Paulist Press, 1979.

Wolpe, David J. *The Healer of Shattered Hearts: A Jewish View of God*. New York: Henry Holt, 1990.

Wood, Ralph C. *The Comedy of Redemption: Christian Faith and Comic Vision in Four American Novelists*. Notre Dame: University of Notre Dame Press, 1988.

Yacowar, Maurice. *Loser Take All: The Comic Art of Woody Allen*. New York: Frederick Ungar, 1978.

Index